A Brief History of the World

Peter N. Stearns, Ph.D.

THE
GREAT
COURSES

D1492844

PUBLISHED BY:

THE GREAT COURSES
Corporate Headquarters
4840 Westfields Boulevard, Suite 500
Chantilly, Virginia 20151-2299
Phone: 1-800-832-2412
Fax: 703-378-3819
www.thegreatcourses.com

Peter N. Stearns, Ph.D.

Provost and Professor of History
George Mason University

Professor Peter N. Stearns is Provost and Professor of History at George Mason University. He received a Bachelor's degree *summa cum laude*, Master's degree, and doctorate in History from Harvard University.

Trained in European social history, Professor Stearns has written books and articles on emotions, childrearing, dieting and obesity, old age, and work as they concern people in both Europe and the United States. He has also written widely about world history, including two textbooks that have gone through multiple editions. He edited the sixth edition of the *Encyclopedia of World History* and is currently editing an *Encyclopedia of Modern World History*. He has written several thematic studies in world history, including *The Industrial Revolution in World History* (2nd ed., Westview, 1998), *Gender in World History* (2nd ed., Routledge, 2006), *Consumerism in World History* (2nd ed., Routledge, 2006), *Western Civilization in World History* (Routledge, 2003), and *Childhood in World History* (Routledge, 2005). His book, *Global Outrage: The Evolution and Impact of World Opinion* (OneWorld) appeared in 2005, and his current interest in using history to understand contemporary patterns of behavior is illustrated in his forthcoming *American Fear* (Routledge, 2006).

At George Mason University, Professor Stearns annually teaches a world history course for undergraduates. He has previously taught at the University of Chicago, Rutgers University, and Carnegie Mellon University. While at Carnegie Mellon, he won the Smith Award for Teaching and Educational Service in the College of Humanities and Social Sciences, as well as the Spencer Award for Distinguished Teaching. He has also worked extensively for the Advanced Placement program, including chairing the committee that devised and implemented the AP world history course (1996–2006). He served as vice president of the American Historical Association, heading its

Teaching Division, from 1995 to 1998. He founded and still edits the *Journal of Social History*.

Professor Stearns was "converted" to world history over two decades ago and has taught it annually since then, first at Carnegie Mellon and now at George Mason. He says he has never encountered another framework that allows him to learn so much without (usually) degenerating into random detail. World history continues to fascinate him; it helps him and his students better understand not only the past but also the world around them. ∎

Table of Contents

INTRODUCTION

Professor Biography i
Course Scope 1

LECTURE GUIDES

LECTURE 1
What and Why Is World History?.......................................3

LECTURE 2
The Neolithic Revolution...9

LECTURE 3
What Is a Civilization? 14

LECTURE 4
The Classical Period in World History 20

LECTURE 5
Cultural Change in the Classical Period 28

LECTURE 6
Social Inequalities in Classical Societies..........................34

LECTURE 7
The Roman Empire and Han China 39

LECTURE 8
The Silk Road; Classical Period Contacts 44

LECTURE 9
The Decline of the Classical Civilizations.........................50

LECTURE 10
The Postclassical Period, 500–1450 56

Table of Contents

LECTURE 11
World Religions and Their Consequences 62

LECTURE 12
The Impact of Islam 68

LECTURE 13
Postclassical Trade and Contacts 74

LECTURE 14
Postclassical Patterns of Imitation 79

LECTURE 15
Western Civilization in World Context 84

LECTURE 16
The Mongol Years 90

LECTURE 17
Civilizations in the Americas and in Africa 96

LECTURE 18
The World in 1450 101

LECTURE 19
The Early Modern Period, 1450–1750 108

LECTURE 20
The World Economy, 1450–1750 114

LECTURE 21
Transformations in Western Europe 121

LECTURE 22
The Rise of Russia 127

LECTURE 23
Asian Empires and a Shogunate 133

Table of Contents

LECTURE 24
The Long 19th Century 140

LECTURE 25
Abolition of Slavery and Serfdom 147

LECTURE 26
Modernization and Nationalisms 152

LECTURE 27
Formation of Latin American Civilization 157

LECTURE 28
China and Japan—19th-Century Pressures 163

LECTURE 29
The 20th–21st Centuries as a New Period 169

LECTURE 30
The World Economy—Change and Continuity 175

LECTURE 31
An Age of Revolutions 181

LECTURE 32
The United States in World History 187

LECTURE 33
Contemporary Democracy 193

LECTURE 34
Contemporary Cultural Change 200

LECTURE 35
Gender in Contemporary World History 205

LECTURE 36
Globalization and World History 211

Table of Contents

SUPPLEMENTAL MATERIAL

Timeline 217
Glossary 224
Biographical Notes 230
Bibliography..233

A Brief History of the World

Scope:

This course presents some of the highlights of the world historical approach to the past, suggesting major changes in the framework of the human experience, from the rise of agriculture to the present day. The lectures cover the emergence of distinct major societies as they deal with common problems but generate quite different institutional and cultural approaches. The course also discusses key changes in belief systems—the emergence and spread of the great world religions, for example—as well as alterations in trading patterns and basic shifts in technology, exploring why some societies reacted differently to technological change than others.

Throughout the course, we will look at many parts of the world, including those clustered into shared civilizations. East Asia, South Asia, the Middle East, and the Mediterranean loom large from the start. Sub-Saharan Africa, where the human species originated, has also played a great role in world history, as ultimately has northern Europe, including Russia. The Americas offer an important variant until their incorporation in global patterns from 1492 onward. Central Asia maintained a distinct position in world history until the 16th century.

World history divides into a limited number of time periods, defined in terms of dominant themes. The rise of agriculture requires a discussion of pre-agricultural patterns. Following agriculture came, in several places, the advent of civilization as a form of human organization. The classical period in world history draws attention to China, India, Persia, and the Mediterranean, when the expansion and integration of these large societies dominated over a millennium of human history. The collapse of the classical empires ushered in a vital postclassical period, when emphasis shifted to religion but also to more ambitious patterns of interregional trade. It was in this postclassical period (500–1500 C.E.) that the emphasis of major societies shifted from separate development to greater interaction and even deliberate imitation. The early modern period highlights a renewed capacity for empire, the inclusion of the Americas in global systems, and—though this must be handled with a bit of care—the rise of Western Europe. What some historians call the "Long 19th Century"—1750 or so to 1914—was dominated by Western industrialization and its economic, military, and cultural impact on, literally, the entire world. Finally, the contemporary period in world history, after World War I, features a bewildering variety of themes that must be sorted out, with emphasis among other things on the relative decline of the West, the huge surge in human population, and the potential for greater globalization.

World history highlights a number of major regions, but it avoids simply examining one area after another—"if it's Tuesday, this must be Latin America"—by making careful comparisons and focusing on interregional contacts. The discipline emphasizes a number of key time periods (though not an indefinite number), defined in terms of basic changes in the ways many societies operated, whether the change was in an economic system—industrialization, for example—or a cultural system, as seen, for example, in the emergence of vigorous missionary religions.

World history also embraces two common themes. First, and most obviously, is the eternal tension between change and continuity—the stuff of history as a discipline. Particularly once the classical traditions are defined, world history can be seen in terms of new forces being met and interpreted by established cultural and institutional systems. Of course, these systems change but never completely and never in exactly the same ways from one society to the next.

The second theme involves a perpetual interplay between local or regional identities, on the one hand, and the attraction or simple inevitability of wider contacts, on the other. Societies began trading at long distances several millennia ago. They received immigrants and diseases and, sometimes, ideas from distant places. But they rarely, at least willingly, simply surrendered to outside influence, and sometimes they battled fiercely against such influence in the name of established values. Over time, of course, and particularly with contemporary globalization, the pendulum shifted toward more outside influence, either willingly embraced or endured of necessity. But the tension has not ended, and assertions of regional identities can intensify precisely because the external framework is so intrusive. World history allows us to trace the main iterations of this tension and to place its current iteration in context—and even, tentatively, to talk about its future. ∎

What and Why Is World History?
Lecture 1

The rise of world history has been one of the most important developments in American history education and, to some extent, scholarship over the past two decades.

This is a course about world history, and what I want to do in this first session is to define the beast, talk about why it's developed so rapidly, talk about some problems that are undeniable in the field, and then turn to a few remaining definitional issues. One of the obvious challenges of world history is the extent to which it can include everything. Indeed, it is fascinating that one can add so many different experiences and places and time periods to one's sense of how the world has developed, but any world history—whether it's a semester course or a two-year sequence or a big textbook—any world history is selective.

There are three major approaches to world history—usually applied in combination—that help scholars decide what topics to focus on. The following three approaches are usually used in combination.

- The first approach involves studying major civilizations to determine how they developed and how they helped define the experience of many people in societies around the world. This approach brings major civilizations together to compare what they share and how they differ.

- The second approach involves paying attention to cases where major societies, including civilizations, come into contact with each other. Scholars look at how this contact occurs and how it changes both parties, using this information as a framework to explore far-reaching changes in the experience of peoples around the world.

- The third approach emphasizes the emergence of broader forces that help define contacts and the experiences of individual civilizations. Such forces include new trade or migration patterns, new disease patterns, and new missionary efforts.

The time periods, in turn, are often delineated by changes in patterns of contact or changes in broader forces, such as the diffusion of new technologies or the emergence of new trade patterns. The time periods we will look at in this course are as follows: classical (1000 B.C.E.–500 C.E.), postclassical (500–1450), early modern (1450 C.E.–1750/1800 C.E.), Long 19th Century (1750–1914), and contemporary.

The rise of world history as an academic discipline has been unusual in several respects. World history emerged more as a teaching field than as a research field. World history also did not develop initially at the most prestigious universities in the United States.

The field of world history is not evenly developed around the world. A great deal of progress has been made in the United States, and interesting work has been done in China and Japan. A few European countries, such as the Netherlands, have developed significant world history programs. But the United Kingdom, although it contributes important scholarship to world history, has yet to introduce the topic in its educational programs.

We also need to look at the debate surrounding the idea of teaching world history. World history inevitably challenges older teaching approaches,

Factors that Increase Interest in World History

- The first factor involves changes in the composition of the American student body. A growing number of students in American universities come from backgrounds that are not American, and there is a demand for teaching that reflects this diversity.

- The second factor is the extent to which the United States, since the 1950s, has become engaged with the non-European world. This engagement logically propels us to look for a historical perspective that gives us some context for understanding the world at large, rather than one important but narrow slice of it.

- The world history perspective can be used to gain a better understanding of crucial historical events and processes.

particularly the tradition of Western civilization. This continues to generate disputes between world history advocates and traditionalists. The Western civilization tradition traces a line of historical development from ancient Mesopotamia and Egypt to Greece and Rome, then on to Western Europe, and ultimately, to North America. This approach asserts that because the United States is part of the Western tradition, its students should pay particular attention to the emergence of Western institutions and values.

Some world historians approach the teaching of world history as an exercise in "West-bashing," but others take a more considered position: It is more important for American students to learn something about the world as a whole, including how the West fits into larger world patterns, than it is to learn about the Western tradition more narrowly.

World historians also argue that the opportunity to learn how the West developed, its distinctive features, and its contributions to the global experience is not lost in the study of world history as opposed to Western civilization. The choice of world history in a teaching program involves a different set of emphases from the Western civilization tradition. Scholars of world history seek to avoid the "West-and-the-rest" approach, which focuses on the Western experience with brief mentions of other societies. The more thoughtful approach looks at Western civilization as one of a number of major civilizations—and not always the most important one.

A second concern about the teaching of world history, raised particularly by historians of East Asian civilizations, is that the field cannot adequately convey the complexities of individual traditions. Chinese history, for example, is so nuanced and complex that it is inevitably simplified if taught as only one part of a broader course.

The third objection, raised recently as some Europeans have attempted to insert themselves into a world history framework, is that the field is somehow yet another product of American imperialism. To some extent, this objection seems to coincide with criticisms of American foreign policy. It may also reflect an understandable anxiety that American world historians would slight the European experience, although most world historians in the

United States make an effort to deal evenhandedly with the experiences of various societies.

In terms of chronology in world history, we need to be aware of three kinds of emphases. The first is the emphasis on origins. In the world history context, this approach pays greater attention to the emergence of human societies, sometimes at the expense of more recent developments. The second approach acknowledges that the greatest contributions of world history scholarship to our understanding of the past apply particularly to the postclassical period (roughly 500–1450) and the time right after the early modern period. The final approach—and the one we will use—views both the early and middle phases of world history as contributing to an active modern period and uses the modern period, in turn, to help understand the world in the present day.

Let us look at an overall framework and a few final definitions for the course. World historians, like any analytically sensitive historians, are interested in the balance and tensions between change and continuity. At times, world history seems to focus particularly on changes, but we will also pay attention to continuities among human societies. The civilizational approach will help

us track continuities and traditions in juxtaposition with new elements in the global framework.

We will look at the tension between developments and identities formed in particular localities or regions and the advantages of contact and exposure to crosscutting forces. We will see that up until about 1,000 years ago, the human experience probably placed more emphasis on the local and the regional than on contact and broader forces. For the past 1,000 years up to today, the human experience places more emphasis on contact and crosscutting forces and less emphasis on local and regional developments and identities, but the tension between the two elements is always present.

This course will look primarily at seven civilizational/geographic areas: East Asia, South and Southeast Asia, the Middle East (and, later, the Middle East and North Africa), Eastern Europe, Western Europe, sub-Saharan Africa, and Latin America.

We will use B.C.E. (Before the Common Era) and C.E. (Common Era) as our main chronological divides. This terminology replaces the traditional use of B.C. (before Christ) and A.D. (anno Domini, "in the year of the Lord") in world history. This convention steers us away from the Christian definitions used in Western-focused history and reminds us that we are operating in a global environment.

We will see different reasons for the choices of certain dates to mark specific periods. World historians conventionally end the postclassical period around 1450 C.E., then pick up the early modern period. The year 1450 C.E. has some relationship to the Renaissance and the Reformation, major periods in traditional Western history, but the year also relates to important developments in the Middle East and North Africa, Russia and Eastern Europe, and in the relationship between the Americas and the rest of the world. ∎

Suggested Reading

David Christian, *Maps of Time: An Introduction to Big History*.

Gerald Danzer, *Atlas of World History*.

Patrick Manning, *Navigating World History: Historians Create a Global Past*.

Peter N. Stearns, Michael Adas, Stuart Schwartz, and Marc Jason Gilbert, *World Civilizations: The Global Experience*, 5th ed.

Questions to Consider

1. Why does world history seem anti-Western to some? Is this a rift that can be healed?

2. One world historian once proclaimed that the field depended on a key principle: dare to omit. But what criteria can world historians use to decide what to omit? Are some parts of the world less important than others? Are some periods of time less vital than others? Can the three basic approaches to world history help deal with the decisions on what to omit?

The Neolithic Revolution
Lecture 2

This session focuses on the rise of agriculture in human history and uses it as a focal point for developments prior to those that we need to know, but also particularly as a framework for developments that will occur after agriculture is introduced.

The rise of agriculture was one of the great changes in the human experience. Many important developments occurred before this, yet the emergence of agriculture was neither tidy nor uniform, and this messiness must be taken into account when studying this period. The fact is that agriculture greatly changed the nature of life for most people around the world. Further, much of what we deal with in world history involves societies that were primarily agricultural. Indeed, the world is still grappling with the legacies of agricultural patterns and the incomplete transition between agricultural and more urban and industrial ways of life.

Agriculture began around 9000 B.C.E. Between the emergence of humans about 2.5 million years ago until about 11,000 years ago, our species was involved in hunting and gathering. This long period between the emergence of our species and the rise of agriculture raises three important points.

Between 2.5 million years ago and about 100,000 years ago, the human species went through a variety of evolutionary phases in different parts of the world. Early versions of the human species originated in East Africa and migrated to different parts of the world. *Homo sapiens sapiens* emerged about 120,000 years ago, and from that point onward, there have been no major evolutionary changes in the human experience.

The human species, even before *Homo sapiens sapiens*, was a tool-using animal, more adept than other species at finding tools for hunting, gathering, or use as weapons. During the Mesolithic era (c. 12,000 B.C.E.) and the Neolithic era (c. 8000 B.C.E.) tool use—and, by extension, domestication of some animals—became increasingly deliberate, setting a framework for the emergence of agriculture itself.

Massive migration is particularly vital to world history. Some thousands of years after the species originated in East Africa, *Homo sapiens sapiens* began to pour out into other regions and, ultimately, around the world. The reason for this migration is simply that hunter-gatherer societies require as much as 2.5 square miles of space per person. By 25,000 B.C.E., *Homo sapiens sapiens* occupied virtually every place in the world that is currently inhabited, except New Zealand, some other Pacific islands, andBermuda.

Human history begins at a point when the species was widely dispersed. As noted in the last lecture, one of the key tensions in world history is the balance between the local and the connected. People were initially spread out in small numbers and inevitably, because of environmental conditions and other factors, formed intensely local cultures and institutions, setting the stage for the current regional aspect of human identity.

The Teaching Company Collection.

Agriculture was introduced about 12,000 years ago (roughly 10,000 to 9000 B.C.E.) when there were, at most, 510 million people in the world. *Homo sapiens sapiens*

Tools from the Neolithic era.

coexisted with other human species, such as the Neanderthals, for a long time. It is not known how *Homo sapiens sapiens* triumphed over other species, but the process serves to illustrate the complexity of the developments that prefigured agriculture.

Let us now turn to the questions of when agriculture was introduced, the complexities of its introduction, and its implications for the future. The introduction of agriculture, sometimes called the *Neolithic revolution*, was a crucial change in the human experience. Some would argue that, other than the emergence of the species itself, the development of agriculture and the later replacement of agricultural economies with industrial economies are the two key developments of the human experience.

Agriculture was "invented" in at least three separate places. The first invention occurred in the northern Middle East/Black Sea region with domestication of wheat and barley. The second invention occurred in South China and continental Southeast Asia around 7000 B.C.E. with the introduction of rice. The third invention was the domestication of corn, or maize, in Central America about 5000 B.C.E. Agriculture may also have been invented in other places, including sub-Saharan Africa and northern China.

By 5000 B.C.E., agriculture had gradually spread and was becoming the most common economic system for the largest number of people in the world. Despite the advantages of agriculture over hunting and gathering, its widespread adoption was slow. One reason for this slow spread was that contacts among relatively far-flung populations were minimal.

Not all regions were suitable for agriculture; some were heavily forested or arid. An alternative economic system based on nomadic herding of animals prevailed for a long time over agriculture in the Middle East, Africa, the Americas, and Central Asia. Agriculture involves settling down, which might not have been attractive to some hunting-and-gathering societies that treasured their capacity to move around.

When agriculture was introduced, it brought massive changes in the human experience. Agriculture involves more work, particularly for men, than hunting and gathering; thus, it redefined and increased the work expectations of human society. Agriculture also redefined gender relations. In most hunting-and-gathering societies, men did the hunting and women did the gathering, but because both groups contributed to the food supply, women usually had some influence in society. In agricultural societies, however, patriarchal systems predominated. The most obvious reason for the increase in male dominance was that agriculture both permitted and required an expansion of the birthrate. Men increasingly assumed the role of principal cultivator of the crucial food crops, resulting in the development of patriarchal societies.

In hunting-and-gathering societies, children had few functions until they reached their early teens. In agricultural societies, childhood and work became more closely associated, and the idea of obedience tended to follow this shift.

The advent of agriculture raises interesting questions about human progress. Despite what many of us learned in grade school, the adoption of agriculture had a number of drawbacks. In some cases, the following three drawbacks affected some groups' willingness to adopt agriculture:

• The first drawback is the introduction of new kinds of inequality, particularly between men and women.

• The second is that agriculture allowed people to settle down into clustered communities, which exposed the inhabitants to increased incidences of epidemic disease.

• The third is that agricultural societies altered the local environment in a way that hunting-and-gathering societies did not do, to the extent of damaging and even destroying a regional environment and the communities that existed there.

The advantages of agriculture, however, allowed it to spread. One not entirely frivolous theory to explain this spread is that agriculture allowed the growth of products that could be fermented to create alcohol. More systematically, agriculture significantly improved food supplies, which in turn allowed families to have more children and resulted in population expansion. These conditions prevailed for a long time, between about 9000 B.C.E. until 300 to 400 years ago.

Agricultural economies were constrained by limitations in the amount of food that a given worker could generate. Even the most advanced agricultural economies required about 80 percent of the population to be engaged primarily in agriculture, which limited the amount of taxation that could be levied and limited the size of cities to no more than 20 percent of the population—a crucial feature to remember about agricultural societies in general. Agricultural societies also generated cultural emphases, especially by encouraging new attention to the spring season and to divine forces responsible for creation.

Agriculture is involved with population growth and the generation of surpluses.

The crucial features of agriculture were its role in population increase and its capacity to generate discernible surpluses, which freed at least some people to do other things, such as manufacturing pottery. As we will see in the next lecture, manufacturing could lead to yet additional developments in the human experience, including the emergence of cities and advancements in other areas of technology. ■

Suggested Reading

Jared Diamond, *Guns, Germs and Steel: The Fates of Human Societies.*

Brian Fagan, *People of the Earth: An Introduction to World Prehistory.*

Chris Gosden, *Prehistory: A Very Short Introduction.*

Questions to Consider

1. Why, despite its obvious drawbacks, did agriculture spread so widely? What common human problems did it alleviate? At the same time, why might many people resist agriculture?

2. Why did we once assume that hunting societies treated women worse than more civilized societies did? Why and how, in contrast, did agriculture increase the inequality between men and women? Why did women put up with this result?

What Is a Civilization?
Lecture 3

The focus of this session is on the emergence of civilization as a form of human organization and the early civilization period in world history, which runs variably in the region roughly from 3500–1000 B.C.E.

After agriculture, the next step in setting a framework for world history is the emergence of civilization as a form of human organization. This is where, in the Western civilization tradition of history surveys, history is usually seen as starting. The first human civilization developed in Mesopotamia around 3500 B.C.E. Three or four other early, pioneering civilizations can also be identified during the next 2,000 years. These civilizations, all of them agricultural, generated a number of key innovations that have not had to be reinvented since. Civilizations did not, however, spread uniformly. Furthermore, many world historians are uneasy about relying too much on civilization as an organizing principle, and although their objections may sometimes be a bit too politically correct, they deserve some attention. The civilization concept is useful and valid, but only if its limitations are also recognized.

The early civilization period in world history runs roughly from 3500 B.C.E. 1000 B.C.E. Civilization first emerged in the Middle East about 5,000 years after the advent of agriculture. Before that time, agriculture had permitted the development of some isolated cities, usually with populations of 10,000 or slightly more. Nonetheless, it is important to realize that agriculture did not quickly or inevitably lead to civilization. Some agricultural societies (for example, in West Africa) reached the modern period without forming the apparatus that we associate with civilization.

The emergence of civilization in the Middle East was preceded by other technological developments in addition to the maturing of agriculture. By around 4000 B.C.E., people in the Tigris-Euphrates valley (that is, Mesopotamia) were beginning to use bronze for weapons and tools. They also used the wheel, which had probably been brought to the region by nomads in Central Asia. The use of bronze improved military and production capacities, but it also imposed requirements for long-distance trade and travel, another feature that marks this early civilization period. The first specific civilization to emerge, again in Mesopotamia, was Sumeria. It would be followed over the next several thousand years by a succession of states, including Babylonia and the states of the Hittites, Assyrians, Chaldeans, and others. The attractions of civilization drew migrants and invaders to the region, particularly from Central Asia.

Sumeria, the prototype of early civilization, generally offered a number of features that agricultural societies without civilization lacked. This civilization benefited from surpluses in agricultural production. In fact, some historians would define civilizations in general simply as agricultural societies that have particularly large surpluses. Sumerian civilization offered features of human organization not present in agricultural economies, including a formal political apparatus with leadership and a certain degree of structure. Civilizations thus are defined as *stated societies* rather than stateless societies.

Another feature of civilization was the existence of cities and increased dependence on cities. Cities mean concentrations of people that can facilitate cultural exchange and technological development. Cities also depend on more elaborate trade than agricultural societies, fostering the development of a merchant class.

Civilizations, beginning with Sumeria, have writing, which enables recordkeeping, is associated with bureaucracies, allows long-distance communication and the expansion of trade, and affects the generation and preservation of knowledge. A procession of civilizations developed first in Mesopotamia; some of these expanded into empires in the Middle East. Civilization emerged in Egypt along the Nile from about 3000 B.C.E. Harappan civilization (so called because Harappa was one of its major cities) originated around 2500 B.C.E. in the northwestern section of the Indian subcontinent in what is now Pakistan, along the Indus River. A fourth center of civilization developed in Asia along the Yellow River, or Huang He, in northern China. Some historians also point to the first civilization in Central America, Olmec, as another early civilization type.

The fact that most of these early civilizations clustered along river valleys was no accident. River valleys provided the most abundant opportunities for agriculture and, therefore, the promise of surplus. To take maximum advantage of river systems, however, required the use of irrigation systems which in turn depended on a high degree of coordination and, possibly, some property definition. Use of the river encouraged a situation in which governments and formal rules would make sense.

Many world historians are uncomfortable with the concept of civilization as a vehicle for studying history. The first objection to this approach stems from the version of the civilization story that is sometimes associated with the Western civilization teaching tradition. This version emphasizes the importance of Egypt and Mesopotamia as the origin of a glorious tradition that would pass to Greece, Rome, and Europe. This view ignores the fact that important early civilizations also developed in other places. This view is also vital to recognizing that Egyptian and Mesopotamian traditions fed not only Greece and Rome but also later elements of Middle Eastern, East European, and African civilizations.

The second objection to the civilization approach is the fact that much of the world, particularly in this early period, did not adopt civilization. Polynesian society, for example, was an agricultural economy that had a definite social structure and elements of a state but no writing and no particularly vigorous cities. Civilization did not spread to areas where hunting and gathering or nomadism prevailed or to some agricultural societies.

The third objection stems from the distinction between civilization and barbarism drawn by civilized peoples. It is quite valid to note that civilizations tend to produce people who look down on others. This is an interesting human phenomenon, but it is important not to adopt those prejudices in looking at civilized and uncivilized peoples.

The final concern with the civilization concept is the fact that what we emphasize in civilizations can distort aspects of the human experience and the kinds of groups that form civilizations. For example, writing changes the operation of states, trade, and knowledge-gathering, but until very recently, most people in civilizations were illiterate. Writing affects the way society is conducted, but it does not describe the majority condition. We have emphasized cities, but all agricultural civilizations had, at most, a fairly small minority of the total population living in cities.

Civilization, as we saw with agriculture, involves a mixture of advantages and disadvantages. Civilizations, by writing rules and laws, formalize the inequality between men and women. Civilizations usually develop a more extensive social structure between the upper classes and the lower classes. Many civilizations extend the capacity for warfare beyond that found in hunting-and-gathering and agricultural societies and, by attracting pressures from the outside, may increase both the importance of military activity and the disadvantages of military activity for ordinary people.

Civilization is, first, a form of human organization, but a second definition of the term involves the emergence and identification of regional characteristics. For example, Mesopotamian and Egyptian civilizations developed close beside each other geographically. They had trade, military contact, and periods of cultural exchange, but the two societies were quite different. The Egyptian emphasis on monuments implies more labor organization and different beliefs about death and the afterlife.

Egyptian hieroglyphics.

Artistic and literary artifacts of the Egyptian culture tend to be somewhat more optimistic that those of the Mesopotamians. At least in the upper classes, Egyptian societies seem to have allowed greater leeway for women. Egyptians did not practice infanticide, as most early civilizations did. These comparisons attest to the extent to which civilizations in this second meaning could develop separate lines of activity, cultural definitions, and political institutions.

The comparative emphasis between Egypt and Mesopotamia highlights civilization as a regionally cohesive force. The same idea applies to other early river valley civilizations. The Harappan civilization seems to have developed elaborate cities with highly advanced urban technologies. Chinese civilization may have placed significant emphasis on the importance of the ruler and the state, at least in comparison to Harappan civilization.

Each of the river valley civilizations had some distinctive features and a distinct history, but they all had essential features in common. These civilizations all had states, established cities, developed trading patterns and a merchant class, and had different kinds of writing. All these early civilizations declined, but what legacies did they leave? The river valley civilizations left societal mechanisms that would never have to be reinvented, including the concept of states, the idea of writing, and the use of money.

It would be nice if all the early civilizations collapsed in April of 1000 B.C.E., and we can say now we're ready for the next [period]. It didn't happen like that … .

These early civilizations left a certain geographic dispersion that would be important later on. Although they concentrated in river valleys, many of the early civilizations had wider influences. Egypt, for example, had interactions with sub-Saharan African societies along the upper Nile that would ultimately generate their own civilizations. Egyptian and Mesopotamian civilizations spread their influence to Greece and Crete.

The third legacy is the extent to which the spirit of early civilizations spread to later societies. The Chinese, in their semi-mythical histories of the Shang dynasty, implied that the Shang introduced the concept of political order that would inform Chinese culture. People have argued also that Mesopotamian ideas about the separation between humans and nature influenced later Middle Eastern and European cultures.

The end of the early civilization period is marked by a hiatus around 1200–800 B.C.E. Harappan civilization, for example, simply disappeared. It was replaced by a period in which Indo-European invaders and migrants poured into India and began to mix with local populations. A new civilization phase and a partial relocation occurred as a result. Egyptian civilization, although it did not disappear, clearly began to falter somewhat around 1000 B.C.E.

The great empires of the Middle East also went through a hiatus in which important local societies emerged, such as Venetia and Israel. This interval was amplified by a new series of invasions and migrations from Indo-Europeans in Central Asia.

Chinese civilization had the least clear disruption; the Shang dynasty flows fairly smoothly into the Zhou dynasty. With the exception of China, this break in civilization history marks the gap between the first civilization period emphasizing river valleys and the classical civilization period that we will define in the next lecture. ■

Suggested Reading

Robert Chadwick, *First Civilizations: Ancient Mesopotamia and Ancient Egypt*, 2nd ed.

Li Liu, *The Chinese Neolithic: Trajectories to Early States*.

Donald Redford, *Egypt, Canaan, and Israel in Ancient Times*.

Questions to Consider

1. Using a defendable definition of civilization, what are its greatest advantages and disadvantages as a form of human organization? Did the arrival of civilization make much difference to the majority of agricultural peoples dispersed in rural villages?

2. What are the key differences between early river valley civilizations and later ones? What did all the river valley civilizations have in common?

The Classical Period in World History
Lecture 4

> The classical period in world history runs from about 1000 B.C.E.—1000
> or 800—to 500 or, possibly, 600 C.E. There's a little fuzziness around
> the edges, but that's the time period. In other words, it's about one and
> a half millennia long.

Almost all world historians define a period running roughly from
1000 or 800 B.C.E. to 500 or 600 C.E. The period saw great
activity and many changes, but it takes its basic definition from
the riseofthree or four major civilizations and the unfolding of their
keycharacteristics, followed by a fairly dramatic decline in each case.
These features do not define the whole world—key parts of northern
Europe, many parts of sub-Saharan Africa, places in Asia (such as Japan),
and the Americas are left out, though they experienced their own
historical developments.

The largest populations centered in the classical societies, and these
societies would also have the greatest impact on later ages, particularly
in their own regions but measurably beyond as well. Although the focus
remains on civilization, classical societies differed in several ways from
their river valley predecessors (whose achievements they all built on).
They also developed a few mutual contacts, a point that must be addressed
even as primary attention goes to the individual classical centers.

The most common way to deal with the classical period is to compare
major developments in each center, such as Greece and Rome. But
before turning to specific results, this lecture addresses a vital preliminary
what the classical civilizations had broadly in common, which is the
same thing as addressing what the classical period as a whole was
fundamentally about.

Some of the key formative elements of major civilizations were forged in
the classical period and would be ingredients in world history from this
point onward. The classical civilizations were situated in areas where river

valley civilizations had flourished earlier, although they usually relocated somewhat and always expanded. China expanded from the north to the southern portion of the Yellow River, forming the Middle Kingdom. Indian civilization spread through the whole subcontinent, with its focus now in the Ganges River basin rather than in the northwest. Classical Mediterranean civilization was located in Greece and along the shoreline of the eastern Mediterranean and ultimately spread westward, both in North Africa and southern Europe.

The classical civilization that stayed closest to its river valley roots was Persia, which had its center in the Tigris-Euphrates valley but also spread more widely in the Middle East. The main purpose of this first lecture on the classical period is to highlight some of the common issues among these four civilizations—China, India, Persia, and the Mediterranean.

We should note two points before we introduce the classical period. First, the world history approach treats Greece and Rome as important classical civilizations, but unlike the Western civilization approach, it does not focus solely on these societies. Second, it is important to remember that the classical world was not yet the whole world. Although the classical civilizations would radiate influence to some other societies, some parts of the world that would be important later on were essentially untouched by classical developments.

Although they all used river valley achievements, these classical civilizations expanded significantly from their predecessors. At its height, the classical Chinese Empire embraced about 54 million people, and classical Rome had about 52 million.

Let us begin by looking briefly at the individual stories of these civilizations in the classical period. From the fairly decentralized, often landlord-dominated Zhou dynasty, China made a move to centralization under the Qin dynasty and even more centralized political and ideological operations under the Han dynasty at the end of the period. Classical Mediterranean civilization emphasized the Greek tradition until the 4th century. This was followed by the period of Alexander the Great's conquests and the Hellenistic period, in which Greek cultural and political influences interacted with the traditions of Egypt and the Middle East. In its final phase, the civilization's emphasis shifted to Rome, the republican period and the empire, which became the most coherent geographic expression of the classical Mediterranean.

In its heyday in the 6th and 5th centuries B.C.E, Persia was far more important than Greece and had established a strong, effective government. The Persian tradition would be partially overshadowed, however, first by the conquests of Alexander, then by the conquests of Arab Islam.

Classical India involves the story of the in-migration of Arian or Indo-European peoples, whose culture was gradually codified into major works of literature and religious philosophy. India, in this second civilization period, settled down into more recognizably coherent development, with a major empire in the 4th century B.C.E—the Mauryan Empire—and, at the end of the classical period, another major imperial statement—the Gupta Empire.

Comparisons of these civilizations highlight some of the crucial differences among the classical traditions as they emerged in this period. Classical China generated Confucianism, the most important ideological statement in the East Asian tradition, as well as Daoism. On the whole, however, China's culture was resolutely secular. Of all the classical traditions, India was the most spiritual, generating Hinduism, Brahmanism, and Buddhism. The Chinese emphasized empirical science because of its clear utility to society and the economy. The Greco-Roman scientific tradition, particularly in the Greek and Hellenistic periods, was noticeably more theoretical. India also had a strong scientific tradition, with an emphasis on the development of mathematics.

Politically, the comparison among the societies is also revealing. Ultimately, the Chinese emphasis would be on a strong central state and an unusually large bureaucracy. Classical China also emphasized key political concepts that supported the central state, a specific training system, and at least the beginnings of an examination system for bureaucrats. India experienced two interesting imperial periods and some other periods when larger political units were formed by invaders.

But the Indian tradition in this period stressed smaller, decentralized states and placed less emphasis on political ideology than either classical China or the classical Mediterranean. The classical Mediterranean had, like China, a strong political emphasis, although its overall political tradition was more decentralized than that of China. The Roman state was somewhat more interested in the development of legal systems as a political unifier, rather than the generation of massive bureaucracies.

Striking social differences arose in India, the Mediterranean, and China. The Indian caste system was probably the most startling social development in the classical period. Caste obligations replaced political obligations in some instances, which helps explain why the Indian political tradition was somewhat less fully developed than was the case elsewhere. Mediterranean society was noteworthy for its strong reliance on slavery, although slavery also existed in India and China. Classical China, under Confucianism, developed a social hierarchy based on the notion of rule by wise people of the upper class, with the lower classes offering deference in return.

China and India offer interesting economic comparisons. Classical China depended heavily on trade, but Confucianism prompted a cultural bias against merchants, who were viewed with suspicion because of their devotion to moneymaking and the possibility that they would pull away from the central political and social values of Chinese society. India placed the most unambiguous emphasis on merchant activities. Merchants were encouraged to use the Indian Ocean as an artery for foreign trade.

Finally, comparisons can be made in the area of technology. In this period and for several periods thereafter, China would be the most important source of technological innovation in the world. For a long time, a pattern was established by which technologies initially introduced in China would gradually percolate westward. India also had a successful emphasis on technologies, particularly steelmaking. The Mediterranean probably had the least well-developed emphasis on production technology, possibly because it tended to expand the slave system rather than increase production through technological development.

This brief overview suggests the possibility of using comparison to highlight some of the interesting differences between these classical societies, but it is not always easy to determine why such different emphases emerged. China may have focused on political order because of its geography. The possibility of invasion from Central Asia may have encouraged an emphasis on order to ward off disruption, but the threat was not so great that establishing political order became impossible.

India was also affected by invasions and influences from the outside world that came through the passes that lead through the Himalayas and northwestern India. In addition, a hoary historical principle holds that India's emphasis on artistic sensuality and religious fervor could have stemmed from its climate. Whatever the origins of these separate impulses and traditions, they would tend to solidify and affect these regions not only during the classical period but well beyond.

The classical period gains coherence from two simple developments. These societies were territorially much larger than their river valley predecessors. China expanded geographically several times over, while the classical Mediterranean coalesced into a unit of its own. The Persian Empire was larger than virtually any of its river valley predecessors. Indian civilization, in spreading through the south continent, embraced a territory vastly larger, more diverse, and more complicated than Harappan civilization had been previously.

Crucial in this expansion was the fact that these civilizations all had access to iron technologies, which were introduced from about 1500 B.C.E. onward. These technologies would serve to underwrite more elaborate and effective production and an expansion of military capacity. Leaders in these societies also saw clear advantages in terms of population expansion to enlarge their economic, cultural, and political territories.

Further, these societies were now comfortable with the apparatus of civilization as a form of human organization, which may have meant that basic developments could be used in combination with new technologies to expand further.

With the partial exception of the Mediterranean, the achievements of these classical civilizations represented fairly durable expansions of their territories. In later periods, China would be truncated geographically, but for most of world history, China is associated with the territory that was established in this period. The same holds for India if we view India as a cultural unit, not simply a political one. The same may hold to some degree for the recurrent reassertions of the Persian commission.

Following expansion, all these societies faced the need to develop an apparatus of integration that would allow the expanded territories to be successfully used and maintained. In China, the government relocated northern Chinese from the Yellow River region into the south to develop population loyalty amid the diverse ethnic and linguistic picture of south China. Rome, in its imperial period, also relocated groups of Roman citizens as well as military garrisons to unify its territory.

We call this period classical because of both the reverence and the fact that it was formative.

The classical civilizations emphasized three basic integrating devices. Perhaps the most obvious device was economic integration. All these societies traded to some extent beyond their borders, but primarily, they focused on economic, communication, and trade patterns that would connect the various parts of the expanded territories. The Chinese promoted regular interaction between the wheat-growing regions of north China and the rice-growing regions of south China, creating canals that would facilitate exchange. Mediterranean rulers and merchants eagerly developed contacts with grain-growing regions, such as North Africa and Sicily.

A second integrating device was culture. In the 6th and 5th centuries B.C.E., all these societies introduced key cultural systems: Confucianism and Daoism in China, Hinduism and Buddhism in India, Zoroastrianism in Persia, and philosophy and art in the Greco-Roman world. These cultural systems were expanded throughout each empire, at least among the elites, to provide something of a cultural glue.

The most complicated device was political integration. In all cases, there was an effort to take advantage of the territorial expansion of the civilization and to build imperial structures that would foster and reinforce economic and cultural coherence. Throughout this period, the imperial tradition was more of a recurring effort than a consistent one.

The result of integration is seen in achievements that later societies in these regions and elsewhere would look back on with awe and reverence. Thus, each of the classical traditions outlived its own existence by creating identities, value systems, and institutions for a variety of societies that would come later on.

We call this period classical because it was both formative and, later, revered. We will see institutions, cultural and artistic patterns, and even economic and technological values crop up later that hark back to the legacy of these societies in this important period in world history. ∎

Suggested Reading

Lindsay Allen, *The Persian Empire: A History*.

N.G.L. Hammond, *The Genius of Alexander the Great*.

Rhoads Murphy, *History of Asia*.

Steven Shankman, *Early China/Ancient Greece: Thinking Through Comparisons*.

Questions to Consider

1. Why did the specific features of the classical civilizations differ so much? Geography clearly played a role—think of the Chinese Middle Kingdom as compared to the mountainous terrain of Greece which encouraged separate city-states. Climate may also have played a role. But what about earlier precedents, such as the Indo-European culture for both the Mediterranean and India, and what about the creativity of individual leaders?

2. What is similar and different about the way a contemporary educated Indian is likely to think about classical India and the way a contemporary educated Westerner thinks about the classical Mediterranean?

Cultural Change in the Classical Period
Lecture 5

> Culture is an obviously vital but slightly elusive part of the human experience. We're talking about culture not just in terms of great ideas or artistic forms but basic beliefs, values, and assumptions.

Creating large and durable cultural systems was one of the hallmarks of classical civilizations. Many people experienced significant changes in basic belief systems as the period unfolded—not an everyday occurrence in human affairs. Confucianism and Daoism in China (along with legalism, which urged tight state control over the people), Hinduism and Buddhism in India (plus some smaller religious strains), Zoroastrianism in Persia, philosophy and art in the Mediterranean, and ultimately, Christianity, increased in importance at the time and have remained important since.

Classical belief systems present two contradictory images, both quite real. First, the factors that reshaped cultures in this period are probably more important than other types of changes, such as political changes. Cultural developments in each of the classical civilizations moved some people away from what had been cultural staples in the human experience up to that point. Second, the most obvious result of cultural change in the classical period was the development of cultural signatures for each of the major civilizations. Without question, sharp distinctions emerged and remain important to this day; at the same time, we will also look at some shared features of culture in the classical period.

Culture, in the sense of basic beliefs, values, and assumptions, is a vital but elusive part of the human experience. Human beings depend heavily on culture because we do not have many basic instincts. One reason for the extended childhood of humans is the need to imprint cultural elements into the psyche.

By the time of the early river valley civilizations, different cultural forms, such as artistic expressions and beliefs about death had emerged. For most people, cultural approaches centered on fundamental features with local variations. It is probably fairly natural in the human experience to have strong initial beliefs in polytheism and magic. By the time of the river valley civilizations, another cultural element was the idea that the rulers of these new civilized states were either directly inspired by gods or were themselves gods. During the classical period, these staples—polytheism, belief in magic, and belief in the divinity of rulers—were not overturned, but they were modified, as we'll see later in this lecture.

The classical period was marked by the emergence of key cultural figures, mainly in the 6th and 5th centuries B.C.E.: Confucius and Lao Tzu in China, Zoroaster in Persia, Socrates and his philosophical heirs in 5th- and 4th-century Greece, and Buddha in India. These figures drew on prior traditions in the regional culture to create coherent and widely appealing statements that helped shape distinct cultural identities in each of the classical areas. Zoroaster, for example, emphasized the importance of the tension between supernatural forces of good and of evil.

Chinese culture was particularly shaped by Confucius and Confucius's interpretation of earlier Chinese tradition. In this culture, the emphasis was on the importance of political order and hierarchy. Confucius believed that people were fundamentally good and, if properly educated, would realize their duties to society as a whole. Classical Chinese culture, however, was also shaped by Daoism, which emphasized the importance of harmony with nature, contemplation, and balance.

Terra cotta warriors from the mausoleum of Emperor Qinshihuangdi.

Indian culture was shaped by the emergence of Hinduism. Indian religion was initially fashioned by the priestly caste, which remained important, but during the classical period, Indian beliefs evolved into a more sophisticated and varied religion. Classical Indian culture was also shaped by Buddhism, which shared many beliefs with Hinduism but quarreled with Hinduism's focus on the caste system and its emphasis on priestly rituals and detailed observances as the proper path to spiritual development.

Classical Mediterranean civilization did not, until the advent of Christianity, produce a major religion. It infused the polytheistic religion brought in by Indo-European invaders with literary representations that exploited the gods and goddesses as ethical models. It also added, increasingly, an overlay of abstract philosophy, including an interest in scientific speculation and the powers of reason.

The classical period, as it was shaped by individual thinkers and by the larger evolution of basic cultural forces, produced distinct cultural signatures that would mark major regions, not only at that time but for some time to come.

All the classical cultural systems were aimed at creating a framework for ethical behavior. In India, for example, whether in Hinduism or Buddhism, the justification for ethical behavior could be found in the spiritual advancement that would result from doing the right thing. The Hindu ethical concept of *dharma* asserts that those who obey their caste obligations in this life will have the opportunity for spiritual advancement in subsequent spheres of existence. This is a direct use of religious and spiritual motivation to underwrite the appropriate ethical code for behavior in this world.

In contrast, Confucianism used a secular justification for ethical behavior, which should be a function of appropriate recognition of the individual's obligations to the larger society. The basic philosophical tendency in classical Greece and, later, Rome was that the reasons for ethical behavior should be found in individual explorations of ethical imperatives and the relationship between the individual and larger social obligations—again, a secular justification.

The most obvious result of the classical cultural systems was to create something of a common language for elites. Elites in China, for example, might individually oscillate between interest in Daoism and interest in Confucianism, but both packages shaped a common elite cultural experience across classical China. The same can be argued for the elite experience in the Mediterranean.

The cultural systems and their elite audience were also reflected in predominant artistic forms. The characteristic restraint and spare depictions of nature in Chinese art relate to Confucian injunctions for personal restraint and emotional control, as well as the Daoist's interpretation of the importance of harmony with nature.

Indian art, perhaps more sensual and vibrant, relates to the Hindu sense of the vigor of individual gods and goddesses as representations of the larger divine essence. Classical Mediterranean art, with its monumentality and its emphasis on balance, correlates closely with some of the predominant emphases in Mediterranean culture more generally. These cultural signatures would be widely recognized by elites and would shade over into the most widely disseminated public art to constitute something of a cultural package. They provided identity within the civilization and some distinctions from outside cultures.

These variations should not, however, obscure some key similarities. All these evolving cultural systems moved, at least to a degree, away from some of the previous staples that had defined river valley civilizations and earlier human experience, including polytheism, belief in magic, and the divinity or divine inspiration of the ruling class. Further, all these classical systems were marked by a certain amount of diversity.

On the whole, the classical period was marked by considerable tolerance. Classical Mediterranean rulers turned against a few specific cultural strands, including Judaism and Christianity, but primarily when these strands seemed incompatible with political loyalty.

These cultural systems were, for the most part, not actively missionary. The one exception in this period is Buddhism. It seems as if the proponents of these systems were aware that they were providing a cultural definition for a civilization, not a statement for humanity as a whole.

That said, classical systems inevitably had some influence beyond the borders of the major civilizations themselves. Confucianism began to have an impact on Korea and Vietnam. Hinduism fanned out with other aspects of Indian influence, particularly merchant activity, to locate Hindu centers in other parts of Southeast Asia.

The most important issue surrounding classical cultural packages is the extent to which they gradually reached out toward ordinary people. Their initial cultural emphases focused on helping to shape a common set of assumptions for members of the governing elite. The clearest beneficiaries of cultural systems were members of the elite, who had the time and resources to indulge themselves and to educate their children in artistic and literary endowments. Ordinary people had a less clear stake in the cultural package.

For example, popular religion in China would continue to reflect a belief in a multitude of divine spirits and use symbolism to help people protect their homes against adverse spiritual forces. The same was true in the classical Mediterranean, where ordinary people continued to participate in folk religions that were undoubtedly polytheistic and had a strong magical content.

The common elements of these classical systems were an emphasis on cultural values that could be widely shared in the civilization.

Of course, the elite value systems developed in the classical period influenced the belief patterns of ordinary people. Certain Confucian values, for example, reached beyond the upper class in China to help ordinary people understand their relationship with the upper classes and to organize their households. The penetration of cultural systems in the Mediterranean focused on artistic forms. Almost certainly, cultural packages spread farthest in India, probably because they were so integrally wrapped up with religious expression. Ordinary people could see in Hinduism or Buddhism hope for spiritual advancement.

We will close this lecture by reemphasizing the balance between diversity and commonality. Diversity is the more obvious feature of classical systems. For example, Chinese people, influenced by Confucianism, would have very different reactions to basic human experiences than their counterparts in the Mediterranean. These cultural systems are not just abstract but describe fundamental reactions to ordinary issues in human behavior.

We can also identify commonalities, such as an emphasis on values that could be widely shared to provide cultural arguments for obedience to the existing social and political order. As a result, classical civilizations all generated value systems that would have lasting impact on the regions in which they were created and, sometimes, well beyond. ■

Suggested Reading

Johann P. Arnason, *Axial Civilizations and World History*.

G. E. R. Lloyd, *Ancient Worlds, Modern Reflections: Philosophical Perspectives on Greek and Chinese Science and Culture*.

Thomas McEvilley, *The Shape of Ancient Thought: Comparative Studies of Greek and Indian Philosophies*.

Questions to Consider

1. Why might ordinary people accept new belief systems emanating from the intellectual and spiritual leaders of the classical civilizations? Were there significant differences in popular appeal in each case?

2. Why, except for Buddhism and, at the end of the period, Christianity, were the classical belief systems not widely exportable to other societies?

Social Inequalities in Classical Societies
Lecture 6

Each of the classical civilizations—and I'll be focusing on China, India, and the Mediterranean—had a somewhat distinctive social system that marked its particular definition of social inequality, and each of the classical civilizations also had a slightly different version of a patriarchal gender system.

All the major classical civilizations not only established great social inequalities but also assumed that inequality was inevitable and desirable. Confucianism argued that both elites and commoners should respect and complement each other, but the culture urged deference on social inferiors. Greek philosophers such as Aristotle wrote about the inevitability of slavery, arguing that it was essential to provide the means for the wise elite—the aristocracy—to govern. The Indian caste system, religiously sanctioned in what came to be Hinduism, marked people off in terms of occupations and permissible social contacts. Similar insistence marked gender relationships, with male superiority clearly defined. These systems of inequality—rather different from what most modern people are comfortable with—raise questions about how much attention ordinary men and women should receive for this long period in world history. Can we just note their presence and marked inferiority and leave it at that?

Each of these classical civilizations had a distinct social system that marked its particular definition of social inequality, and each also had a slightly different version of a patriarchal gender system.

Such social systems are an important aspect of our sense of the past. Ordinary people have a historical legacy of their own, and they matter in terms of the legacy of the larger societies in which they existed. Social experiences and structures are relevant to the framework of world history as a whole. Some historians might argue that because they were marginalized, ordinary people, perhaps women in particular, should not take up too much of our attention. We will look at arguments for why the inequalities of these civilizations should be more than simply a matter of record.

Each of the classical cultural systems provided explanations for why social inequality was both necessary and justified. The Greek philosophers argued that slavery was essential for the conduct of society because only with slavery could sufficient production occur to support the upper class. Confucius put forth a similar argument. A minority of people in the upper classes (the gentlemen) would be wise and able to govern well; they owed these dispositions to the lower classes. Hinduism made the social inequality statement quite directly: different people are in different social layers. Those who act appropriately in the current social layer will earn the possibility of spiritual advancement.

None of these systems was designed to justify inequality, but they all did so. In contrast to the modern world the classical world, especially the elites of the classical world, clearly saw social inequality as essential. Nonetheless, these social systems were not as rigid we might imagine.

The caste system of India, for example, seemed inflexible, but levels of wealth could vary considerably within a caste. There were also subgroups within castes called *jati*, and one could move among these with much greater ease than among castes. In the Mediterranean slave system, slavery could involve extremely harsh working conditions, but more slaves were involved in domestic service, tutoring, and even running stores and shops. Confucianism urged a distinction between gentlemen and ordinary people, but it was possible for a bright peasant boy to gain an education and achieve a position in the imperial bureaucracy. None of these systems was as static in practice as it might seem in theory, although mobility among classes was not common.

With some exceptions, many social groups, although technically unequal, did not have routine daily contact with one another. Peasants, for example, were certainly subject to exactions by landlords, but on a day-to-day basis, the landlords were not their employers in the modern sense. Indian historians have argued plausibly that the caste system was not characterized by routine interference. If you followed your caste obligations and did not try to assume inappropriate relationships, you might be left with substantial opportunity to observe your own group culture and maintain group contacts.

The gender systems of classical civilizations were patriarchal. Many classical societies—particularly China and Greece—depended on quite high rates of female infanticide.

Just as with the system of social inequality, however, the system of gender inequality must be seen through the lens of the individual civilization. All the classical civilizations were patriarchal, but not all of them were patriarchal in the same way. In classical China, where Confucian culture was actively used to describe appropriate family relationships, the family was a mirror of society; thus, the older father in the family was the emperor, and women, as a subordinate group, were to be productive and deferential.

In India, Hindu legalists debated the question of whether a woman who lived up to her obligations in this life would advance to being a man in the next life. In classical Greece, upper-class women were confined to the household. Rome was somewhat more lenient; the patriarchal strictures there, at least for a few centuries, were probably the least severe.

How did women tolerate these distinctive gender signatures? Patriarchy tended to isolate small groups of women in separate households, so women didn't have much opportunity to gather in groups and compare notes. Women were themselves victims of the dominant culture. They were told that they were inferior, and many of them internalized this notion. Individual women could be forceful within the patriarchal system. Ban Zhao, writer of a manual specifying how women should behave in classical China, was herself an educated, upper-class woman. Patriarchal strictures operated with greatest force in the upper classes. In the lower classes, inequality was less marked because men and women knew that both parties were essential to the economic survival of the family.

Two additional points are crucial to the question of how women survived the system. Although women were inferior in the patriarchal system, they were not the outright property of men. In all the patriarchal systems, there was a certain possibility of leeway over time.

Why do all these different systems of class and gender matter? Some scholars have argued that different versions of patriarchy could produce different male behavior. The importance of different social systems is even more obvious in the area of technology.

The technological levels of classical China and the classical Mediterranean differed considerably. The Mediterranean was known for its civil engineering and construction, while China excelled in practical technological innovations in the area of production. These differences may be explained, in part, by differences in government or cultures, but the most obvious explanation is that if the Chinese wanted to improve productivity, their most obvious recourse was to invent a new technological device. When landowners in the Mediterranean wanted to improve productivity, their most obvious recourse was to acquire more slaves. The social system helps explain different production arrangements, different technological experiences, and, as we will see in the next lecture, different foreign policies.

Obviously, some of the assumptions and systems involved in patriarchy, although presumably now eroding, continue to be influential, as well.

It is certainly likely that the classical Chinese civilization faced the greatest degree of recurring social protest; the civilization that probably faced the least was classical India. Classical China nested social inequality in a Confucian culture that insisted that hierarchy had to be leavened by reciprocal benefits. The system of inequality, combined with the cultural system, thus produced situations of unrest, in which the peasants thought their actions were justified by the value system. Classical India reinforced the caste system with religious rewards and sanctions. Because social groups were kept partially separate in the caste system, they did not interact as directly as landlords and peasants might in China. Social cultural systems also matter in terms of the attachments ordinary people developed to their societies and social order.

The legacy of the classical social systems was both specific and general. India still grapples with remnants of the caste system, even though it has been outlawed for more than half a century. Elements of Confucian social thinking still mark the Chinese experience. Slavery systems are officially gone, but the influence of classical thinking about slavery certainly marked history. Some of the assumptions involved in patriarchy, although now eroding, continue to be influential as well. The larger legacy that we continue to contend with is the extent to which inequality was assumed and deeply embedded in economic systems, access to literacy, and political rights. ■

Suggested Reading

Moses I. Finley, *Ancient Slavery and Modern Ideology*.

Peter N. Stearns, Erick Langer, Lily Hwa, Merry E. Wiesner-Hanks, Paul Vauthier Adams, *Experiencing World History*.

Bella Vivante, ed., *Women's Roles in Ancient Civilizations: A Reference Guide*.

Questions to Consider

1. How much attention should we pay to social systems and ordinary people in trying to understand the classical civilizations, compared to the more familiar focus on great thinkers and rulers? Did the social systems of the classical period leave legacies for later ages?

2. Why did women not rise up in protest against their inequality in all the classical civilizations? What combination of repression and opportunity best explains their substantial public silence?

The Roman Empire and Han China
Lecture 7

This session talks about the comparison between the Roman Empire and the empire of the Han dynasty in China. The purpose is several-fold. First of all, quite simply, it's a terrific comparative opportunity.

The several centuries of success for Han China (202 B.C.E.–220 C.E.) and the Roman Empire (27 B.C.E.–476 C.E.) pinpoint possibilities for comparison in the classical period. They can also help an American audience combine more familiar knowledge, usually about Rome, with an appreciation for less familiar classical achievements, as in China. Both empires provided relative peace over wide areas, organized vigorous internal trading networks, and created immensely potent political systems. Elements of their achievement—Roman law, for example, or the Chinese principles of bureaucracy—would shape world history even to the present day. But the empires were also different, for example, in military and expansionist outlook and in cultural integration. These differences would affect the ultimate legacy of each empire.

Comparing the Roman Empire and the Han dynasty reinforces the idea that the world history approach must be balanced. These empires did not exist throughout the whole classical period, nor were they the only significant classical societies.

The Han dynasty and the Roman Empire each lasted more than 400 years. Both empires ruled large masses of territory in orderly fashion for a considerable period of time; the population levels of the two empires were also remarkably similar, with more than 50 million people each. Both empires had clearly emphasized territorial expansion prior to the advent of these regimes.

Both empires strove for economic integration. The Han continued the policy of building roads and canal systems to link major parts of the empire, which in turn, allowed specialization and trade among the major regions. Rome sought to establish granaries in Sicily, North Africa, and elsewhere that it could then reach through Mediterranean trade routes.

Both empires worked directly for political integration using slightly different mechanisms. In Han China, several devices combined to produce a political structure capable of ruling a vast empire. The Han dynasty attempted to further Confucian thought as a means of inculcating certain values in the elite and, possibly, other classes. The emperors continued a tradition of emphasizing their divine or semi-divine majesty. Finally, the Han introduced the first clear system of bureaucracy, in which the central government designated representatives in the provinces.

Rome had its own methods of attaining political integration. Many Roman writers, particularly early in the empire, were eager to sing the praises of the emperors and the imperial system.

Rome developed a somewhat more rudimentary bureaucracy than the Chinese, but the Romans placed more emphasis on the legal system and the rule of law across the empire. Rome did not usually assert the divinity of the emperors themselves but surpassed the Han in imperial monuments, triumphal processions, and emphasis placed on the majesty of the emperor.

Both systems also expanded the functions of government, using their considerable powers of bureaucracy and taxation to provision major cities. Both governments were actively engaged in a certain level of economic activity designed to ensure a stable social and political order.

The differences in these two systems still seem to fall within a context of remarkable similarities. The Chinese regime worked harder at integrating its vast territory than the Romans. The Middle Kingdom in China in the classical period was the scene of major ethnic mixing and division, particularly in South China. The regime tackled this head-on by planting large colonies of northern Chinese in the south and by encouraging the common use of Mandarin at the elite and bureaucratic levels. Some of these policies are still conducted in frontier regions by the Chinese regime today.

Rome planted colonies of soldiers that could begin to foster the Roman lifestyle in remote provinces. These were smaller colonies and not intended for population integration. The Romans encouraged the use of Latin by the upper class, although it never managed to erase the predominance of Greek in upper-class circles in the eastern Mediterranean. The Romans emphasized the expansion of Roman citizenship. Despite these integrating devices, Rome was content to establish looser control over most of its provinces and to rely on local autonomy.

There's an interesting final difference between the two stories—a story of remembrance and selective utilization versus a story of revival.

Both the Roman Empire and Han China underwent significant territorial expansion, but China was capable of surviving a cessation of expansion and was more willing to deal with borderline territories than Rome. The Han Chinese pushed the boundaries of empire out well beyond the Middle Kingdom, but when they had reached a sustainable point, they did not feel the need to compensate for the cessation of expansion.

Rome's appetites in this regard seemed to have been less clearly bounded. One reason for this may be that the Mediterranean value system was, quite simply, more militaristic than the Chinese. The Romans needed additional territory as a means of rewarding generals and soldiers. The Romans needed expansion to provide a continuing supply of slaves to the labor system. Rome more clearly began to decline when it reached the point at which expansion became impossible, after about 180 C.E.

Han China was unquestionably the more culturally creative of the two empires, while Rome's literature, art, and architecture—at least until the imperial conversion to Christianity—tended to derive more from earlier Greek experience. Classical China was also more creative in the area of technologies, particularly production technologies.

Before the Han dynasty, classical China created basic philosophical and religious systems in a way that Rome did not. Neither Han China nor classical Rome developed or sustained cultural systems on their own that satisfied the spiritual needs of important segments of the population. The Han dynasty's emphasis was on Confucianism, while classical Rome's emphasis was on civic religion. Both emphases called attention to rituals and themes that would bring loyalty to the imperial system, but neither system was intensely spiritual. In Han China, Buddhism began to draw interest in the later stages of the dynasty and would surge forward after the dynasty collapsed. In Rome, increasing numbers of Romans converted to Christianity.

Both Rome and China encouraged military activity. The Roman system depended on tight military discipline and the careful organization of infantry in the Roman legions. The Chinese military was probably best known for its approach to military philosophy. It is from the Han dynasty that we get the *Art of War* by Sun Tzu, one of the great works on military thinking generated by any society.

The two empires obviously had different origins. The Han dynasty sprung more directly from earlier dynastic activity in classical China, replacing a period of disorder under the Zhou dynasty with a focus on the importance of political order. Rome's origins in politics had more to do with the control of aristocratic landlords and the importance of a certain democratic element in Roman politics, both of which were overridden by the institutions of the empire.

Both empires began to fade as the quality of individual emperors declined, as the empires faced invasions from Central Asia and elsewhere and suffered from increasing economic stagnation and from disease that reduced overall population levels. Once the western stronghold of the Roman Empire fell, the empire would be remembered and borrowed from by later regimes but would never be reconstituted. The Han dynasty was destroyed but its institutions and achievements were revived by later regimes. ■

Suggested Reading

Constance A. Cook, *Defining China: Image and Reality in Ancient China.*

James I. Porter, *Classical Pasts: The Classical Traditions of Greece and Rome.*

Callie Williamson, *The Laws of the Roman People: Public Laws in the Expansion and Decline of the Roman Republic.*

Questions to Consider

1. What were the greatest similarities between the Roman Empire and the Han dynasty? Why did classical India—just as successful a society by many measurements, including economic prosperity—not develop a comparable great empire?

2. It is no secret that Rome would ultimately collapse more completely than the political system of Han China, which proved to be revivable though without the Han dynasty itself. Were there distinctive features of the Roman approach to empire, compared to the Han, that help explain this result?

The Silk Road; Classical Period Contacts
Lecture 8

This is a discussion about contacts among civilizations and regions during the classical period. Of all the discussions we're having about the classical world, this one is perhaps the discussion that would most please the pure world historian because, as we discussed in the first session, world historians love to talk about contact.

There is no question that the classical civilizations focused primarily on their own development—on the demanding task of trying to integrate unprecedented stretches of territory economically, culturally, and often politically. We have noted before that world historians feast on contact. It is also true that important contacts among classical civilizations developed that were significant both at the time and in their implications for the future. Trying to understand these contacts and to balance their intriguing qualities with their clear limitations provides another angle on the main features of the classical period and its relationship to later ages. This lecture focuses on two types of contact: trade contact and direct juxtaposition between two civilizations.

Before we begin to discuss contact between civilizations, we should note that the classical period is defined by regional history, not local history, and by connections that expanded those regions systematically and, in some cases, durably. We will explore the contact that overlaid these regional integrations, while not overshadowing the regional picture. In other words, the regional focus remains primary; wider contact is a significant overlay. Two major types of trade contacts developed during the classical period, the most famous of which involved the contacts along the Silk Road.

The Silk Road was a nexus of trade routes that ran from western China, usually through Central Asia, across the northernmost reaches of the Himalayan Mountains, into the Middle East through Persia, and sometimes beyond the Middle East and into the Mediterranean. Alternative routes took some trade through India. Trade along the Silk Road took traders into a variety of ethnic settings, particularly in Central Asia. It frequently involved direct interaction between merchants from established agricultural economies and nomadic traders. As the name implies, the good that was most important on this trade route was silk, manufactured in China and increasingly esteemed by people in the Middle East and the Mediterranean. Flowing along the Silk Road in the other direction were exotic animals, gold, slaves, and to a lesser extent, spices and food products from points along the more easterly end of the chain.

What was the significance of the Silk Road? The increasing taste for silk in the Mediterranean is an example of the ways in which new patterns of trade can feed consumer interest. The trade was economically important for some manufacturing centers in western China and, obviously, for the merchants. In other respects, however, this trade pattern did not have a major impact on the economies of any of the major societies involved.

Trade along the Silk Road proceeded in stages along the expanse of the Asian continent. Nobody, as far as we know, traveled the length of the route from the Mediterranean to China or vice versa. This fact, along with the relatively light volume, helps explain why the Silk Road did not generate particularly intense cultural or technological exchanges.

A second nexus of trade developed with India as its center. This network involved trade from the Middle East and the Mediterranean going directly to India, as well as Chinese interest in direct trade with India. By the time of the Roman Empire, regular expeditions were mounted annually from the Red Sea to the subcontinent of India, and colonies of Roman merchants operated in some southern Indian cities; the key interest here was spices, such as pepper.

The trade was sufficient to motivate some government encouragement as well as the desire to acquire better knowledge of navigation. We can also assume some direct involvement between the Mediterranean and Indian societies. Chinese trade also reached India, both along the Silk Road and over the sea, from the Pacific coast of China to the Indian Ocean and eastern India. As trade centers, both India and the Silk Road remind us that classical civilizations did not operate in complete isolation. They increasingly learned the advantages of at least limited commercial outreach.

Some other trade routes developed that pressed beyond the boundaries of the classical civilizations themselves. China developed a fairly robust trade with Korea and Vietnam. India had probably the most extensive trade outreach of any of the societies; merchants from southern India, in particular, traded with other parts of Southeast Asia, including modern Indonesia. Mediterranean and Middle Eastern traders developed contacts with parts of sub-Saharan Africa. Active trade also connected Ethiopia with the Middle East and points in the eastern Mediterranean. Thus, the classical civilizations, along with their strong emphasis on patterns of internal trade and commercial integration and specialization, reached out for certain products to a wider network that embraced territories beyond the classical civilizations themselves.

The classical period offers our first stories of great interregional travelers. In this period, for example, the 5th-century Greek traveler Herodotus recorded his stories, revealing an active imagination, curiosity about distant places, and tolerance for diverse habits and practices. Herodotus also, however, illustrates some of the continuing limitations of interregional contacts; he went to Egypt, parts of the Middle East, and into the western reaches of Central Asia, but by later standards, his travels were a bit modest.

Herodotus and other early travelers were willing to mix absolute nonsense with solid fact. At the end of the classical period, a series of Chinese travelers moved into Central Asia and India, where they often sought Buddhist sanctuary and inspiration.

A second kind of contact beyond travel and trade emerged through encounters between major civilizations. The first of these was the encounter in the 6th and early-5th centuries B.C.E. between Greece and Persia. This was an unusual situation, in which two major societies, operating on different cultural and institutional bases, had direct territorial and military interaction with each other, resulting in mutual learning and mutual antagonism.

Alexander the Great's conquests brought Greek civilization into more extensive contact with societies and cultures in the Middle East, including Persia and northwestern India. Emissaries from Hellenistic societies interacted directly with representatives of Indian culture with several interesting, although limited, results. There was an artistic interaction that followed this period of Hellenistic-Indian contact and lasted for about 150 years. There was an exchange of ideas between Greek and Indian mathematicians. Alexander's intrusion into India possibly inspired later Indian leaders to begin greater political and imperial activity on their own. Possibly fueled by this contact, some Buddhist missionaries were sent into the Middle East, where there was some interaction with Middle Eastern ethical thought.

A final contact began to take shape from the 2nd and 3rd centuries C.E. onward between China and India. China began to import Buddhism directly from India, along with Buddhist artistic styles and literature. Large numbers of upper-class and ordinary Chinese converted to Buddhism. This contact was mediated by an effort to ensure that Buddhism was consistent with the Chinese value system. Buddhist statements about the value of celibacy and individual spiritual quests were recast to make this aspect of the belief more harmonious with Chinese values. These religious adjustments illustrate the idea of symbiosis in exchanges between civilizations, that is, a combination of the imported value system with beliefs and practices from the receiving society in a syncretic fashion.

So the contact points in the classical period are well worth noting. They're an important and subsidiary part of the classical story.

Despite these patterns of contact, the basic "stuff" of classical history continues to be the individual civilizations and the areas immediately around them that they could affect through trade and cultural exchanges. For most of the classical civilizations during most of this period, direct borders with other large, organized civilizations were the exception rather than the rule. Greece abutted Persia, and the Roman Empire would have contact with Persian kingdoms and war with them, but large stretches of the Roman Empire bordered on hunting-and-gathering or early agricultural societies, not on highly organized civilizations. Most of China's borders, with the exception of Korea and Vietnam, similarly involved contacts with nomadic peoples, not those of other civilizations; the same applies to much of India.

Classical history remains a history in which contacts are an important but secondary story. These contacts were marginal in terms of the leading economic themes in the major regions; they did not generate durable cultural influences that touched more than one society and did not develop patterns of technological diffusion. Nonetheless, the exchanges were significant enough that they would be remembered even after some of the apparatus of the classical period fell into disuse.

The Silk Road network, particularly, had depended on effective Chinese control of a territory that reached into Central Asia. These routes also depended heavily on the organization of Persia that was first achieved in the Persian Empire and then revived by successor states. As the classical societies began to decline, the importance of trade opportunities and, possibly, even the promise of cultural exchange remained vivid enough that people would actively seek replacements. For this reason, the contact points in the classical period are well worth noting. They did not overwhelm the greater dominance of factors operating within the civilizations, but they helped to inaugurate a phase in which new types of contact would be pursued and new levels of contact would develop in succeeding centuries. ∎

Suggested Reading

Andrew Bell-Fialkoff, *The Role of Migration in the History of the Eurasian Steppe: Sedentary Civilization vs. "Barbarian" and Nomad.*

Jerry Bentley, *Old World Encounters: Cross-Cultural Contacts and Exchanges in Pre-Modern Times.*

Milo Kearney, *The Indian Ocean in World History.*

Frances Wood, *The Silk Road: Two Thousand Years in the Heart of Asia.*

1. What were the main benefits of contacts beyond individual civilizations in the classical period? What benefits—that we are accustomed to expect from contacts—did not widely occur at this point?

2. Why weren't the classical civilizations even more interested in contacts with one another?

The Decline of the Classical Civilizations
Lecture 9

The fall of one empire, however significant, might not mark the end of a full world history period, but the fact is, the fall of the Roman Empire was joined in approximately the same chronological span by the fall of the Han dynasty in China and, slightly later, the fall of the Gupta Empire in India.

Strikingly, within a period of about 400 years (from the 2nd to the 6th centuries C.E.) these great classical empires collapsed. If the emphasis of the classical period had been on the expansion and integration of large territories, clearly, the period was now coming to an end. The pattern raises vital questions of causation: What forces pushed once-great societies into decline? Are we dealing here with a law of history, that societies have some kind of common lifespan that pushes them ultimately into aging and decay? These questions must also address another vital feature of the period of classical decline, that although there were some common processes at work, the results were quite different from one case to another. This differentiation helped set the framework for the next period of world history, and it, too, must be explained.

These declines had, if not global, at least Afro-Eurasian dimensions involving significant changes in some of the structures that had been developed in the classical period. In looking at the fall of these empires, we should note that they all had experienced significant ups and downs in the classical period.

In the Mediterranean, the Greek city-states reached an apogee at the end of the 5th century and then went into a period of decline. This was followed by the Hellenistic period, the Roman Republic, and the Roman empire. In Indian history, the fall of the Mauryan Empire was followed by a period of regional emphasis, then by the rise of the Guptas. Chinese classical history had been marked by the decline of the Zhou dynasty over a long period. These earlier oscillations all occurred within a persistent framework, so that we can point to change but not to a major termination of the period. In contrast, the fall of the classical empires involved a significant alteration in political and, in many cases, economic and cultural structures, after which the world would be measurably different.

In this lecture, we will look at three separate stories, beginning with the Han dynasty. The Han dynasty entered a period of greater weakness toward the end of the 2nd century C.E., marked by interruptions in Han rule, deteriorating economic conditions, and social unrest. The Hun invasions finally toppled the empire, and it no longer existed after 220 C.E.

The Teaching Company Collection.

The Roman Empire reached its high point around 180 C.E., after which it became impossible for Rome to expand further. Over the course of the 3rd and 4th centuries and, finally, in the 5th, the quality of leadership in the empire deteriorated, and the army began to intervene more crudely in political affairs. Rome's internal trading network began to deteriorate in favor of local economic emphases and efforts at self-sufficiency. In turn, the central state was

Alaric, chief of the Visigoths led the army that sacked Rome in 410 A.D.

unable to collect as much tax revenue as it had earlier. These conditions were followed by a period of invasion, especially from Germanic tribes on the northern border of the empire. The Roman Empire officially ended, at least in the West, around 476 C.E.

The Gupta Empire in India began to deteriorate in the 5th century. Emperors were unable to control local rulers, resulting in decentralization. In the 6th century C.E., a group of Huns from Central Asia dislodged the empire altogether.

These three cases span a period of almost 400 years, from the 3rd century to the 6th century C.E.; by the year 600, the classical world was essentially gone. To have such similar developments occur this close together suggests that we can identify some common processes and common results in the situations of these three civilizations.

We can easily point to commonalities in the process. All three empires found themselves less able to function. The qualities of central leadership deteriorated. Local political and economic elements began to take center stage. Economic performance stagnated. In some cases, social unrest increased in response to worsening conditions. All of this was capped by a series of invasions.

Scholars have generally identified three coincident factors in the fall of these empires, the first of which was invasion. In China and India, the attacks of the Huns were directly responsible for the end of the empires. In the Roman Empire, the direct invaders were for the most part Germanic tribes; these tribes were pushed into Roman territory partly because of invasions from Central Asia by the Huns.

The second factor was an increased incidence of disease. These epidemics may have been smallpox or measles, probably spread from India. Both the Roman Empire and China experienced economic and social dislocation brought on by massive death. Labor was difficult to find, and people pulled back from the more elaborate production and trade arrangements that had marked the empires at their height. Governments had difficulty collecting taxes. Local landlords would compensate for their revenue decline by increasing pressure on local populations.

The third causal factor in the decline of these empires involves human qualities. Less talented leaders were a factor in the decline of the great empires, especially in Rome. There was an increased selfishness on the part of elites, who became less willing to serve in government or military positions. The morale of ordinary people may also have deteriorated.

Do successful civilizations inevitably go through periods of infancy, maturity, and decline? This notion of a humanlike pattern of existence for major societies was posited by, among others, the British world historian Arnold Toynbee. Civilizations seem to reach a height that they cannot sustain because their bureaucracies become more venal, more defensive, and less interested in the innovation that created the vitality of the civilization in the first place. The success of the system carries the seeds of its own destruction.

Some observers today have wondered whether these laws of history and the analogy of the fall of the great classical empires may apply to societies today. The idea of laws of history must be modified for the classical period by a recognition that the fate of the different civilizations varied from one case to another, despite the similarities we have seen so far.

The fall of the Gupta Empire in India, for example, was followed by a long period, literally centuries, in which no large empires were created in India except as a result of Muslim and, later, British invasion. The next time an Indian state was created by Indians was the Indian democracy in 1947 after the departure of the British. Hinduism and the Indian caste system continued to spread. India's trade activity worsened a bit in ensuing centuries, but India remained a productive economy. The fall of the Gupta Empire was a significant change but did not mark the decline and fall of the civilization.

The Chinese case involved real social and political dislocation. The fall of the Han dynasty was followed by 350 years in which central government institutions did not operate. China was divided politically into regional entities, and landlord power increased. In the sixth century C.E., however, the short-lived Sui dynasty was established; with it, came a period in which China recovered most of the institutions and cultural values of the Han dynasty. The idea of decline and fall of Chinese civilization would be misleading; there was a major interruption, but it did not destroy the capacity to reinstate earlier institutions.

The fall-of-civilization image applies most accurately to western Rome. The authority of the state dwindled, and localized conditions prevailed. When the civilization revived, it did not do so literally according to Roman dimensions. In the eastern empire created by Constantine, the Roman civilization was replaced by the Byzantine Empire, which maintained many of the institutions and cultural attributes of Rome.

Thus, we do not know from classical history whether the maturity of civilizations will result in a massive change in the capacity of social institutions or a period of dislocation, followed by revival. Either path can be illustrated by events in the classical period.

Instead of asking why we see decline and fall, we should ask why we see differential decline and fall. One factor is that invasions might be more or less severe, as was the case with the greater pressure of the Germanic tribes on the western part of the Roman Empire. At the same time, India was probably less affected than China or Rome by new disease patterns. It is also possible, particularly in the Roman west, that the institutions and values of the empire may have been less deep-seated; thus, the attachment between ordinary people and the empire may have been weaker.

> **The deterioration of … economic and political decline … inevitably helped push people to think about cultural alternatives to the kinds of political values that had described the classical period.**

Three durable changes constitute the reason we use the fall of the great empires to mark the end of one period and the beginning of another. In much of the civilized world, the emphasis on empire diminished. Societies were less capable of maintaining large, integrated political structures, were less interested in doing so, or both.

The deterioration of this-worldly conditions inevitably pushed people to think about cultural alternatives to the political values that had described the classical period: the end of the classical period and the beginning of the next period would be marked by a greater religious emphasis.

The changes in the Roman Empire resulted in what seems to be a permanent division of the Mediterranean world into three entities: Western Europe; the northern Middle East/southeastern Europe; and the rest of the Mediterranean coast, including North Africa. This division marks the next phase of world history and continues to mark world history up to the present day. ■

Suggested Reading

Jared Diamond, *The Rise and Fall of the Third Chimpanzee: Evolution and Human Life.*

William McNeill, *Plagues and Peoples.*

David Shotter, *The Fall of the Roman Republic.*

Norman Yoffee and George L. Cowgill, *The Collapse of Ancient States and Civilizations.*

Questions to Consider

1. What, on balance, does the late classical period teach us about some sort of inevitable law of societal decline? Why should societies collapse after success, and is this a pattern that the late classical period demonstrates?

2. What was the relationship between classical decline and the spread of Christianity and Buddhism?

The Postclassical Period, 500–1450
Lecture 10

> We're talking today about the postclassical period in world history and its general contours. It's a period that runs from about 500–1450 C.E. You could argue maybe a little later. You could argue 1450, give or take, but we're talking about roughly, not quite, a 1,000-year span of the human experience.

World historians increasingly use the neutral term *postclassical* for this crucial period; the European term *Middle Ages* or *medieval* makes little sense for the world at large. At first glance, this period can seem particularly confusing. Both the number and geographical range of civilizations increased, leaving us without the convenience of three or four focal points, as in the classical period.

One reason for this confusion is that the geographical territory organized into civilizations in this period expanded greatly, as did the number of separate civilizations. A second explanation stems from the European history term for this period, the *Middle Ages* or the *medieval period*, which somehow implies an awkward, stagnant stretch of experience in Europe between the grandeur of Greece and Rome and the glories of the Renaissance. On reflection, however, we can focus on two or three larger themes.

First, the period saw the spread of the three world religions—Buddhism, Christianity, and Islam—with the latter the most dynamic during this millennium. Hundreds of thousands of people, from Ireland to Japan, from Sweden to the Swahili coast, changed their basic beliefs.

Second, the pace and impact of international trade accelerated. The Indian Ocean became the key artery for world trade, but it was supplemented by north-south routes from Africa and Europe, by increased activity along Asia's Pacific coast, and of course by contacts through the Mediterranean. Dramatic innovations in religion and trade, then, set the tone for the period. Every society in Afro-Eurasia had to react to these new forces, though their reactions varied.

In the process, world history gradually changed from an emphasis on the separate development of key societies (divergence) to the interaction and frequent deliberate imitation among key societies (convergence). The year 1000 C.E. can be taken as the basic dividing line. Developments later in the period, particularly the brief but decisive establishment of the Mongol empires, enhanced the pattern of convergence. The postclassical period thus not only offers coherent focus but constitutes one of the crucial transitions in the human past.

From a world history perspective, the postclassical period was a time of great dynamism, with many major innovations and extremely vigorous societies. Medieval Europe would be only a small part of this larger experience. In trying to define the postclassical period, we are using a key analytical tool of historians, periodization. The introduction of a new period in world history means that the framework that had described the human experience previously is no longer central.

In introducing a new period in history, we must address three points. First, we need to prove that the themes of the previous period are no longer dominant. Second, we need to say when the new period comes into play and when it stops being salient. Finally, we need to articulate what the new themes are to which most major societies will have to react.

The first point in this instance is easily established. With the fall of the great classical empires, we no longer see the processes of expansion in China, India, and the Mediterranean and the development of integration devices in these societies to hold their expanded territories together. At the end of the classical period, China and India are essentially established. We certainly do not see continued expansion and integration in the classical Mediterranean because that civilization has burst apart.

The second point we must address in introducing a new period relates to chronological boundaries. The beginning of the postclassical period is marked by the fall of Han China, Gupta India, and the Roman Empire.

The period is also marked by the emergence of the Arabs and Islam as a new force in world history, beginning around 600. In this period, Arab-Islamic civilization becomes the first world-class civilization that we have dealt with in world history thus far. The end of the postclassical period is described primarily in terms of Arab political deterioration but also changes in Arab cultural and economic roles. This reduction would be followed by perhaps two centuries of experimentation, resulting in some intermediate systems that take us up to 1450.

The postclassical period saw the emergence of a larger number of civilization centers and a larger geographical range for civilization than had been true in the classical period. The Mediterranean world split apart and three related but distinct civilizations emerged from the wreckage of the Roman experiment. The first of these developed in the Middle East and North Africa, which became the heartland of Islam and the Arab world. The second involved the territories carved by the Byzantine Empire in the northeast corner of the Mediterranean and the extensions of Byzantine influence into other parts of Eastern Europe. The third involved the society that we have come to call Western European society.

New territories entered the civilization game, including Japan, Russia, northwestern Europe, northern Germany, the British Isles, Scandinavia, additional parts of sub-Saharan Africa, and the Americas. The splitting of the Mediterranean world and the geographical expansion of civilization brought with them new challenges in defining the number of civilizations in our study.

Two themes serve as primary focal points for the postclassical period. The first theme involves the spread of world religions, which showed the capacity to pour across political and cultural boundaries without necessarily erasing those boundaries. These world religions—Christianity, Buddhism, and Islam—would push so far into the civilized regions of Afro-Eurasia as to touch literally every major society.

The postclassical period is partly defined by the immense surge of missionary religions, mainly originating in the Middle East or India, but spreading from these places to other parts of Asia, much of Africa, and ultimately, almost all of Europe. This focus on cultural developments helps explain why the postclassical period is not defined by overarching political themes.

Churches, networks of Islamic centers of law and scholarship, and Buddhist temples become the focus of activity in this period, eclipsing the role of formal states.

The second theme involves the emergence of a "world network." In this period, systematic exchanges begin to predominate much of the Afro-Eurasian world. During the postclassical period, a basic commercial artery emerges, running from the Middle East across the Indian Ocean to India and Sri Lanka, reaching Southeast Asia, stretching into the Pacific, touching the Philippines, and extending to the Pacific coast of China. This east-west artery was embellished by an elaborate series of feeder routes that ran north to south—linking China, Africa, Scandinavia, and northwestern Europe to the Arab world. These trading connections were sustained by new technologies, new navigational devices, and improved map making.

> Though they sometimes coexisted, sometimes even tolerated each other magnificently, the religions did set up some new cultural boundaries that could modify or challenge the new commercial connections.

One other mechanism useful for interpreting this period is a categorization of the new and old centers of civilization into one of three economic and contact zones based on their relationship to new patterns of interregional trade. The first of these zones is focused on the Arab world, the Byzantine Empire, India, and China. In the language of today, this zone would be the developed world—the areas that built most clearly on the achievements of the classical civilizations. These areas had the most sophisticated manufacturing systems, the largest cities, the most sophisticated, opulent upper-class and artistic styles of life, and the most elaborate political structures. These areas traded actively with and influenced one another.

Around these centers emerged a host of societies in which civilization was a relatively new form of human organization—including Japan, parts of Southeast Asia, sub-Saharan Africa, Russia, and northwestern Europe. These societies forged trading connections with the more developed regions.

Deliberate imitation enabled these second-tier societies to develop cultural and economic apparatuses more quickly than they would have otherwise. A third significant region of civilized experience, which we'll discuss in later lectures, also developed in this period but had no effective contact with either of the first two zones.

The two major themes of this period raise some final points. The spread of world religions involved new kinds of contact, rivalry, and suspicions that would become durable parts of the world history environment. At the same time, many world historians would claim that the new trade connections and the resulting contacts and imitation possibilities deserved even greater emphasis.

One world historian has said that around the year 1000 C.E., the human experience reached a crucial divide. Before that time, the bulk of human experience was shaped by local and regional factors, with the focus more on separate factors instead of shared ones. After 1000 C.E. the balance shifts, with a focus on convergence rather than divergence. From that point to the present, one sees a pattern of interaction, a thirst for contact, and a willingness to imitate that transcend the divisions and local identities that had been emphasized earlier.

We can see the importance of new levels of contact, but the concomitant development of new religious loyalties sets up an obvious dilemma; religions established new cultural boundaries that could modify or challenge the commercial connections.

In sum, one emerges from the postclassical world with a sense of new contact and interaction but also with the potential for new rivalries. These divisions would shape the world of the postclassical centuries and the world after that as well. ■

Suggested Reading

Janet Abu-Lughod, *Before European Hegemony: The World System, A.D. 1250–1350.*

Ross Dunn, *Adventures of Ibn Battuta, A Muslim Traveler of the Fourteenth Century*.

Patrick Manning, *Migration in World History*.

Questions to Consider

1. What are the main differences between the world around 1200 C.E. and the world around 100 C.E.? What are the main differences, in others words, between the postclassical and classical worlds at their respective high points? Are there also some important continuities between these two worlds?

2. What are the signs of growing convergence among major societies during the postclassical period? What were the main reasons that this growing convergence occurred?

World Religions and Their Consequences

Lecture 11

Our focus today is on the spread of world religions during the postclassical period. I said in the last session that the spread of religion was one of the two great themes of this period, a theme to which virtually every society in Afro-Eurasia had to respond.

Although two of the three world religions originated earlier—in the case of Buddhism, much earlier—the postclassical period saw the crucial geographical expansion of Buddhism and Christianity, as well as the origins and expansion of Islam. Conditions of the late classical period help explain the new religious impetus.

By 1450, with a few exceptions, the religious map of Europe, North Africa, and Asia was set in terms that survive today. Christianity had yet to reach the Philippines and Korea, of course, and Islam's penetration of Indonesia was just beginning, but otherwise durable changes had already occurred. Expansion was accompanied by compromises with existing belief systems. Nevertheless, enough cultural change occurred that not only religious life but also economic activity, social relationships, politics, and artistic and broader intellectual efforts were deeply affected. This spread of religion would have common results in areas as diverse as gender relations, law, and art.

We will try to remain value-neutral as we look at religion, but we may encounter some pitfalls, particularly in justifying the selection of Buddhism, Christianity, and Islam as world religions. In the postclassical period and after, each of these religions has shown the capacity to persuade people beyond conventional political boundaries and cultural zones that it represents the truth. Identifying these three faiths as world religions does not mean that they are the "best" religions; many other religions were and are important in world history. When we say that these three world religions took geographical shape and exerted much of their influence in the postclassical period, we are not denigrating other major faiths.

From a historical standpoint, three factors caused the spread of world religions. The first of these is context. Although Buddhism, Christianity, and Islam began at different chronological points, their takeoff periods related to the collapse of empires in the later classical period. As economic levels deteriorated, political instability grew, and the population saw new levels of disease and death, people looked for institutions to compensate for the decline of the state institutions. This situation offered a compelling framework within which missionary religions could take hold.

The second factor involves the quality of missionary activity, which in all three cases, was often correlated with expanding merchant activity. Merchants, through their commercial success, as well as their geographical outreach, helped bring religion to new areas. Missionaries, as they sought to convert new souls, frequently established a framework for new commercial activity.

The third factor involves the extent to which one or more of the world religions could seem associated with other aspects of success. In all three religions, individual rulers adopted the faith not just for themselves but for their subjects. In the process, they used the religion to cement loyalty between the people and the state. Religion might also be associated with commercial success. Converting to a particular faith offered the opportunity to trade with new sources of wealth.

The chief change with these new religions was a replacement of polytheism. People stopped believing in the old sets of gods and goddesses and started believing in one of the more unifying, more abstract, religious sources. This process of conversion involved compromise. All the world religions, formally or informally, made some bargains with polytheism. They might, for example, build new religious institutions where old temples had been or incorporate hints of the old gods and goddesses in rituals of veneration for other holy figures. These adjustments come under the name *syncretism*, that is, the extent to which in accepting new beliefs people hold onto remnants of the old.

Buddhism, as it fanned out from India, took two major directions, with a third at least briefly noteworthy. Buddhism began to lose ground to Hinduism in India proper. Many Indian rulers saw in Hinduism clearer support for military and commercial activity, and they distrusted the abstract quality of Buddhism.

As Buddhism faded in India, however, it gained ground elsewhere. It spread to Southeast Asia and, at the end of the early postclassical period, to China, Korea, and Japan. The Chinese embraced Buddhism, with the stipulation that Buddhism adapt to Chinese modes of thought. Buddhism would also exercise an impact on other Chinese belief systems, such as Daoism. The Tang dynasty in the first part of the postclassical period ultimately turned against Buddhism on the grounds that Buddhists were unreliable allies of the state and too foreign to Chinese values.

Sculpture of Buddha.

The spread of Buddhism to other parts of East Asia was less qualified and would exert a longer-term influence than the spread in China. There was a Buddhist surge into Central Asia and, belatedly, into Tibet. Buddhism showed an impressive capacity to adapt to local conditions and to tolerate and merge with other aspects of the local religious scene.

The story of the spread of Christianity may be somewhat more familiar. Christianity fanned out widely in the Roman Empire after the death of Christ, largely based on missionary activity. This spread involved not only the European parts of the empire but also Armenia, North Africa, parts of the Middle East, Persia, and other parts of Asia. The Emperor Constantine's decision early in the 4th century to tolerate Christianity represented a significant opportunity for Christian advance. By the end of the century, Christianity was a state religion.

Christian expansion after the fall of Rome took two main paths. In Eastern Europe and the northern Middle East, the Byzantine Empire sponsored orthodox missionaries who went northward into East-Central and Eastern Europe. Western missionary activity fanned out to Britain, Germany, Scandinavia, and Poland.

During the postclassical period, Islam reached larger territories and more peoples than either of the other two missionary religions. Islam spread rather quickly among Arabs and some others in the Middle East and North Africa. It also spread widely in India and Central Asia. Toward the end of the postclassical period, Islam began to make major inroads in Southeast Asia, particularly in Indonesia, which is now the largest Muslim nation in the world. Islam also had success in parts of southern Europe and sub-Saharan Africa.

What were the differences in these three world religions? Unlike Christianity and Islam, Buddhism was not clearly a religion of the book. It had a less well defined relationship to state authorities and was more hostile to things of this world. At the same time, Christianity and Islam differed on the nature of the divinity, how salvation could be obtained, how religion should be organized, and degrees of tolerance.

Thus, the spread of world religions introduced a new differentiating factor into world history in Afro-Eurasia—a differentiating factor whose ramifications continue to apply to the present day.

These religions also had some common effects that help describe larger processes of change

The world religions had, then, some common effects on not just patterns of belief but larger cultural expressions, introducing new political and social tensions … .

during the postclassical period and beyond. The spread of world religions increasingly set the framework for artistic and philosophical activity. These religions defined the leading artistic and architectural work in much of Asia, Africa, and Europe. Much work was devoted to questions about how older philosophical systems and scientific discoveries fit with the new sense of religious truth.

Particularly for Islam and Christianity, the religions also reshaped the framework for law, dividing it between secular and religious activities;

the notion that law was a state matter was jettisoned as the religions developed bodies of legal work and commanded jurisprudence. All three religions raised new questions for the state itself: If these religions carried primary truth, what was the role of the state? Should the state be reshaped mainly to defend religion? Was there some way to separate political and religious areas of activity? What was the relationship between religious and political authority?

The rise of world religions might seem to introduce a new tension between value systems and trade. If the main purpose of existence was otherworldly, too much attachment to material objects and motivations would be wrong. Nonetheless, the world religions also, in their own ways, encouraged trade.

Each of the world religions also carried an important social message— although, again, a complicated one. On the one hand, the religions all posited the fundamental spiritual equality of all believers; on the other hand, they argued that social inequality and poverty would always be facts in this world. The main point of religious life was not to fight the social system because that would distract from otherworldly goals. The world religions modified the casual acceptance of inequality that described the classical period, but none of the religions crusaded against social inequality.

The same bifurcation applies to gender. Each of the three world religions clearly specified that women had souls alongside men, and each provided new opportunities for women in religious vocations. Nonetheless, the world religions also sustained and even, in some cases, increased the institutions of patriarchy. During this same period, new institutions arose that coexisted with the religions and extended women's inequality (for example, foot binding in China and *sati* in India).

The world religions also faced a choice between hostility and tolerance toward other religions. There are certainly examples of new levels of intolerance. For example, Chinese authorities attacked Buddhism, while Christians and Muslims clashed during the Crusades and the Christian Reconquest of Spain. There are also surprising islands of mutual toleration in the postclassical period. For example, many parts of the Middle East saw significant Christian and Jewish communities remain, even as Islam spread.

Muslim Spain tolerated, even encouraged, interactions among the three basic religious faiths. The choice of tolerance or intolerance was not fully addressed in the postclassical period, though new questions were raised. ∎

Suggested Reading

Peter Brown, *The Rise of Western Christendom: Triumph and Diversity, 200–1000 A.D.*

Denise Carmody, *Women and World Religions*, 2nd ed.

Richard M. Eaton, *India's Islamic Traditions*.

Questions to Consider

1. What were the main causes of the spread of the world religions? What role did decisions of political leaders play?

2. What impact did the messages of spiritual equality have on the lives of women in the patriarchal civilizations?

The Impact of Islam
Lecture 12

> The rise of the Arabs and Islam was clearly one of the most important developments during the postclassical period, and three major facets of this need to be emphasized.

The spread of Islam broadly fits within the larger patterns of expanding world religions. Islam and the Arab society involved with it, however, clearly gained a particular importance and power position during the postclassical period. The religion had special impact as a result, some of which would continue long after the postclassical period ended. Further, Islam is so hotly debated today that some special attention is warranted from that angle. Unlike the other two world religions in this period, Islam interacted with literally all the civilizations in Afro-Eurasia during the postclassical centuries. Its implications for trade, politics, and social relationships were similarly far-reaching. Islamic society also experienced important changes in its Middle Eastern/North African heartland, adding to the complexities of its role in postclassical world history.

The surge of the Arabs from their original homeland in southern Arabia into much of the rest of the Middle East and across North Africa created a new civilization zone that remains influential to this day. An Islamic religious zone was established that ran from Morocco in Spain across the Middle East through India, on to Indonesia, and even to the southern Philippines. This zone also spread south into Africa.

Even for those regions that did not directly convert to Islam, the power of the Arabs and their religion inevitably compelled attention. China, for example, encountered the Arabs and Islam in its western provinces. Russia, although not in this period Islamic, was also quite aware of the importance of Islam. Western Europe encountered Islam directly as the Islamic invasions poured into Spain and parts of Sicily.

In discussing Islam, we must address some of the complexities associated with it. In the contemporary world, Islam encounters biases because of participation of some Muslims in terrorism. Further, Westerners have, for a long period of time, harbored prejudices against Islam that have led to outdated and exaggerated perceptions. Islam covers vast territories and encompasses many variations beyond the Shiite-Sunni split.

We begin our discussion with the complicated relationship of the Arab military and commercial surge after 600 and the simultaneous Arab conversion to Islam. In the power vacuum left in the Mediterranean world after the fall of the Roman Empire, Arab leaders saw an opportunity to expand their military efforts, seize new territories, and gain wealth and political power. Their advance would help spread Islam. Most scholars now agree that this Arab surge should be read as largely an interest in new opportunities rather than a sign of Islam's spur to conquest and conversion. Nonetheless, as the Arab world expanded, Islam grew with it.

The Teaching Company Collection.

The spread of Islam during the postclassical period

Vladimir The Great.

was wide-ranging. Islam's extension into India primarily involved efforts by missionaries and merchants, but Arab and Muslim armies periodically poured into India during the period. Islam also penetrated Central Asia, often displacing Buddhism in the process. In sub-Saharan Africa, a mixed Arab-African Islamic community developed along the Indian Ocean coast. In the West African kingdoms, such as Ghana and Mali, Islam became a significant minority faith, mainly among the upper classes. Finally, of course, Islam gradually spread to Southeast Asia, both to the continent and to the islands of present-day Indonesia, where it would ultimately gain a substantial hold.

Why was the Islamic religion so successful? Islam developed clear codes of conduct that outlined the major obligations one could fulfill to gain religious reward in the afterlife. Islam also gained ground simply because of the example of Arab and Muslim commercial, political, and military success.

An interesting combination of tolerance and inducement may also have prompted some conversions in the postclassical period. Jews and Christians were, in principle, people of the book. But Jews and Christians were also subject to distinctive taxation policies. This framework offered some fiscal and political reasons to convert. Relatively few people were forced to convert to Islam. A framework of political activity in which non-Muslims experienced inequalities, however, could be influential.

Certain social groups might be motivated to convert to Islam. Merchants would find that Islam was the most tolerant of commercial activity. Poor people could see in Islam a statement of spiritual equality and an opportunity for access to charity.

Complexities in the spread of Islam involve the famous split that occurred relatively soon after Muhammad's death between *Shiites*, who were attached to a son-in-law of Muhammad as caliph, and the majority *Sunnis*, who held to a different selection procedure for caliph. This rift, based on other patterns of religious interpretation also, began early and continues to define the Muslim world. The emergence of Sufism created another kind of tension between an emotional version of Islam and a more rational approach.

Muslims in the postclassical world, particularly Muslim cultural figures, faced some tensions between the injunctions of the faith and the rich artistic and intellectual heritage of the Middle East. In the Arab world, Muhammad's injunction against artistic representation of animal or human figures (as potential sources of idolatry) was largely upheld, but the Persian artistic tradition continued its earlier experience with human and animal representation.

Islamic attitudes toward music were complicated: the Middle East developed a vigorous musical tradition, although the religion advised against the use of music because of its potential as a distraction from purer spirituality. Much philosophical effort was devoted to the relationship between Islamic faith and rational science and philosophy; building on Greek and Hellenistic traditions, the Arab world generated important scientific and medical discoveries, but there was also the question of how much truth could be gained by reason alone

.The role of the state in Islam was crucial. Islam had a clear model of an ideal ruler, who would uphold the laws and obligations of the religion and use the state to advance Islam. Despite this belief, the Arab caliphate—the rule that was established after Muhammad—was rarely inspired primarily by religion. Like Christianity, but perhaps a bit more forcefully, the Koran urged that even when the state was inappropriately organized or unjust, loyal Muslims should not become embroiled in political disputes because doing so would distract from one's religious obligations. There was the possibility, however, that Muslims might periodically measure the state against the expectations of religious purpose and find it wanting.

One crucial difference between Islam and Christianity is that Christianity was born outside the state. Persecution of Christians in the Roman state was sporadic but present for more than three centuries. Because of Muhammad's position as political and religious leader and the subsequent traditions that shaped the caliphate, Islam was born in association with the state and could be seen more clearly as an instrument of politics. At the same time, Islam was also forced to develop a structure that would allow it to endure even amid state indifference and, at times, hostility: centers of Islamic scholarship and law were organized, which sustained and provided coherence to the religion.

The caliphate finally fell in the 13th century, but Arab society more generally maintained a great deal of vitality.

Islam had important social implications that specifically illustrate some of the larger points about world religions in society, particularly with regard to slavery and issues of gender. Middle Eastern society had a significant number of slaves, yet Islam was not entirely comfortable with slavery, particularly when the slaves were themselves Muslim or had converted to Islam. Although Islam tolerated slavery, it also provided some protections, particularly for Muslim slaves. This was an area of ambivalence in which issues of belief clashed with social reality in ways that were not entirely tidy.

Muhammad unquestionably believed that he was improving the conditions of women as he spread the religion among the Arabs. Several injunctions are particularly noteworthy. The Koran specifically inveighs against female infanticide; indeed, the spread of the world religions generally reduced infanticide throughout much of the Afro-Eurasian landmass. Women were given clear legal rights in Islam, including property rights, divorce rights, and access to worship and travel. Nonetheless, Islam did not provide equality for women. Further, in the Middle East, Islam became overlaid with the acceptance of other regional traditions, notably, the practice of veiling.

Arab society declined in some measurable ways by the 13th century. The caliphate became less effective. Various territories in North Africa and Spain peeled off, even aside from the Christian attack on Islam in Spain. The rich philosophical and artistic discussions that had occurred earlier tended to narrow in favor of greater insistence on religion alone. The Arab role in politics declined as more minority peoples, including Turks, were incorporated into political life. The Arab role in international trade was increasingly disputed.

This decline, however, did not mean the erasure of Arab-Islamic culture or institutions. The caliphate fell in the 13th century, but Arab society more generally maintained a great deal of vitality. Because of the earlier vitality of the Arabs and Islam, this decline marks an important transition toward the end of the postclassical period as a whole. ∎

Suggested Reading

Leila Ahmed, *Women and Gender in Islam: Historical Roots of a Modern Debate.*

Ira Lapidus, *A History of Islamic Societies*, 2nd ed.

Charles Lindholm, *The Islamic Middle East: Tradition and Change.*

Questions to Consider

1. What are the principal similarities and differences between historical Islam and historical Christianity? Why and in what ways did the relationship to the state differ between the two religions?

2. How does the Arab decline compare to the decline of the classical civilizations? How does the ongoing role of Islam affect the terms of the comparison?

Postclassical Trade and Contacts
Lecture 13

It's a different world by the 11th and 12th centuries in terms of the impact and involvement of many people—merchants, consumers, upper-class leaders—the involvement of many people in a dependence on and enjoyment of contacts with distance places.

The increase of interregional trade in the postclassical centuries created and reflected a number of changes. An unprecedented range of areas became involved in what we now call international trade. While still focused heavily on luxury products, the amount and variety of trade changed as well, and new consumer tastes emerged. Trade brought other changes, for example, in shipping technology, mapping, and new opportunities for travelers. New contacts promoted missionary religions but also exchanges of technologies and other systems. It is possible to interpret this surge as the basis for the steady acceleration of trade activities that would ultimately produce globalization.

The new range and intensity of contacts was, along with the spread of world religions, a crucial development in the postclassical period, affecting most of Asia and many parts of Africa and Europe. In this lecture, we will look at the emergence of world travelers as a byproduct of these new patterns of contact, along with the major routes and consequences of contact.

In the 14th century, one of the greatest world travelers was Ibn Battuta. Battuta was born in Morocco in northwestern Africa to a middle-class merchant family. He launched his travels with a pilgrimage to Mecca. In his lifetime, Battuta's travels would take him to Mecca and other parts of North Africa, the Middle East, Persia, Central Asia, India, island groups in the Indian Ocean, Southeast Asia, China, and sub-Saharan Africa.

Battuta's accounts of his travels both reflected and encouraged the new range of geographical contact that was then possible. He was motivated to travel by his religious faith, his desire for sexual encounters, and a massive curiosity about different places.

In addition to illustrating the potential for geographical expression of human curiosity, Battuta's accounts reflect other noteworthy features. He judged his destinations by the standards of Islam. He praised religious piety but deplored departures from the norm. In his one clear venture well outside Islam, his visit to China, Battuta praised Chinese society and cities, but was disoriented without the presence of an Islamic overlay.

Another great traveler of the postclassical period was Marco Polo, the Venetian who presumably went to China under Mongol rule and reported on what he found there. We are not sure that Marco Polo actually went to China. His uncles visited China, and he may have used their accounts, along with Persian travel literature, to fabricate a version of his own travels. If Marco Polo did not travel to China, other Europeans clearly did, sometimes returning via the Indian Ocean and thus encountering South, Southeast, and East Asia. The European travelers differed from Ibn Battuta in one respect: they were less uncomfortable in settings outside their religious orbit.

Combining the cases of Ibn Battuta and Marco Polo (or Polo's uncles), we get a sense of the extent to which people visited distant places. By their accounts, these travelers spurred others to seek new trade and contact opportunities. Travel in this period differed greatly from what had been possible in the earlier classical era. The travelers went farther and encountered far more different situations, and their accounts are much more consistently accurate than earlier ones. These changes reflect a different world.

Let us now turn to the patterns of contact. The core route for the new pattern of contact that emerged in the postclassical period was an Indian Ocean route connecting western Asia or the Middle East with South Asia, Southeast Asia, and the Pacific coast of China. This series of routes was initially forged by Arab merchants primarily, but they were soon joined by Muslims and others from India, Southeast Asia, and elsewhere, and by a number of Persians. These routes carried a variety of goods. Particularly important were manufactured goods from China, such as silk and porcelain, and spices from Southeast Asia or India. This Asian-centered trade pattern spurred major manufacturing expansions, particularly in China. Some historians have even referred to a Chinese industrial revolution during the Song dynasty, which opened in the later-10th century.

Other routes fed into the east-west contact. Two routes connected sub-Saharan Africa to this east-west trade, carrying African goods into the Middle East, North Africa, and other parts of Asia. Another feeder route developed from Scandinavia through what is now western Russia and Ukraine, passing through Kievan Rus on its way to the Byzantine Empire and then connecting with Arab trade. Western Europe also eventually connected with this trade route as merchants from England, the Low Countries, and France traveled over land or along the Atlantic coast to the Mediterranean, the Middle East, and beyond.

A number of important consequences can be seen from these trading patterns. This level of interregional trade had a significant impact on internal economies, particularly the economy of China. Some areas of the world—again particularly China—began to orient part of their economic activity toward production for what we would call world markets.

New kinds of consumer dependence developed as well. Certain elements of the upper classes in a number of societies developed tastes for goods that could be supplied only from distant regions. As West Europeans, particularly noblemen, participated in the Crusades, they learned of the higher living standards common in Middle Eastern cities and developed a taste for that lifestyle. Postclassical Europeans found that they preferred sugar to honey and sought to acquire access to regular supplies of sugar.

This kind of consumer attachment spurred shipping activities in the Mediterranean that would link Europe to Middle Eastern ports where products could be transshipped from elsewhere in Asia. Not all societies were equally susceptible to consumer needs. China, for example, needed far fewer products from the outside world than did Western Europe.

Another important consequence involves new levels of culture contact. A large number of words began to pass into European languages from Arabic, denoting the products (such as oranges or sugar) that were being transshipped from other parts of the world to Europe. Other kinds of cultural exchange were even more important, particularly the widespread adoption of what Europeans called the Arabic numbering system. Mathematical systems spread widely. Algebra (another Arabic word) and Arabic mathematical innovation began to spread from the Arab world to other societies, including Europe.

Technologies were affected by new levels of world trade in two ways: new trading activities encouraged the development of new technologies, and increased trade accelerated the transmission of technological inventions. The Arabs introduced developments in sailing ships, and, toward the end of the postclassical period, the Chinese introduced gigantic oceangoing vessels (junks). The compass was probably invented in China, but its use spread. The Arabs learned about paper in their military interactions in Western China; Western Europeans learned about paper from contact with the Arabs.

An important consequence of new trade patterns was the growing utility that societies in Asia, Africa, and Europe found in maintaining or increasing their commitment to international activities.

There are historians … who will argue that this evolutionary approach, a pattern of interregional connections from the postclassical period blossoming steadily and gradually into globalization, is the wrong view.

The postclassical period was a watershed in world history as interregional connections developed and solidified by 1000 C.E. onward. Many societies in Afro-Eurasia turned from an emphasis on largely separate developments with connections to other regions to an increasing focus on the benefits of connections, the possibilities of imitation, and the possibilities of diffusion.

There is a fairly straight line from the interregional connections that developed in the postclassical period to what we now view as globalization. Of course, contemporary globalization involves far more rapid interactions and a greater volume of trade connections and far more extensive cultural interactions. Still, people who traded, traveled, and wrote travel accounts in the postclassical period inspired others who would extend interregional trading activities still further. Some historians argue that an evolutionary approach to the issue of globalization is misguided. Globalization, in their eyes, is a much newer phenomenon. Nonetheless, the postclassical explosion of trade and travel looms large in world history. ∎

Suggested Reading

Janet Abu-Lughod, *Before European Hegemony: The World System, A.D. 1250–1350.*

Milo Kearney, *The Indian Ocean in World History.*

Tansen Sen, *Buddhism, Diplomacy and Trade: The Realignment of Sino-Indian Relations, 600–1400.*

Questions to Consider

1. During centuries when many people devoted themselves to one or another of the otherworldly religions, how could the interest in trade spread so widely? How can these two postclassical themes be reconciled?

2. What are the main advantages and drawbacks in thinking about this period as the dawn of a globalization process that continues to the present day?

Postclassical Patterns of Imitation
Lecture 14

We'll talk about Japan, Russia, Southeast Asia, and briefly, Western Europe. The main focus is on patterns of imitation that these four areas conducted—usually fairly deliberately—with adjacent regions that were, in some measurable senses, better developed.

Many societies in which the apparatus of civilization was fairly new used the opportunity provided by contacts with neighboring older societies to copy aspects of culture, technology, and social structure. This is a further illustration of the importance of the new interregional network, though the imitations were on a regional rather than a global level. Japan, Russia, and Western Europe provide examples of the process, which includes other cases, such as Vietnam and Korea in East Asia and the Southeast Asian importation of religious and artistic forms from India, China, and later the Middle East. Imitation helps provide some common themes and comparative opportunities for the otherwise diffuse process of civilization expansion. It also raises questions, however, about civilization definition: Was Japan part of a larger, Chinese-dominated East Asian civilization, or did it remain so different from China that it should be handled separately? How is Russia to be treated in relation to other parts of Christian Europe? Finally, the process of imitation did not extend well to politics, where attempts to copy larger government models largely failed in favor of more decentralized systems. Here, too, is a common dynamic among the imitative societies, though a somewhat negative one.

Early in the postclassical period and continuing for at least a century, Japan organized expeditions to China in search of trade and knowledge. The Japanese came to imitate China in an impressive range of sectors. The Japanese learned new agricultural and manufacturing techniques from the Chinese that spurred development of the Japanese economy. Japan also took up much of the culture and cultural apparatus of China, including its writing system, basic verse styles, martial arts, the art of gardening, and Buddhism; with Buddhism came architectural forms such as the pagoda and temple.

Chinese social ideas were adopted in Japan to a limited extent. The prestige of merchants declined slightly in Japan. The Japanese did not import the full range of Chinese thought about gender relations, but they did learn from the Chinese that women were less equal to men than the Japanese had previously believed.

Japan adopted something of China's superior attitude toward the wider world. One reason that the Japanese did not attempt a larger expansion effort in this period may be that their horizons were limited by the idea that they had nothing to learn from places other than China.

Trade ran through western Russia and the Ukraine during the postclassical period, connecting Russia with the Byzantine Empire. Russians traveled to Constantinople for political missions and cultural exchange, and Byzantine emissaries were active in Russia. The Russians got their writing system and religion from the Byzantine Empire. Along with religion and writing came a larger cultural apparatus conditioned by the extent to which Russia was a less prosperous, less sophisticated society than Byzantium. Byzantine architectural styles were imitated, along with the Byzantine tradition of iconography. From the Byzantines, Russian leaders incorporated at least some sense of political horizons. A kind of historical chain was believed to link Rome to Byzantium to Russia.

Japan and Russia exhibited similarities in the basic process of adoption and adaptation. In each instance, people in the imitating society believed that there was a positive advantage in visiting and copying aspects of the adjacent, more prosperous society.

This process raises a question that is crucial for the postclassical period: now that civilization is expanding and societies are deliberately imitating each other, how do we define a civilization? In the Japanese case, Japan imitated China, but it did not become Chinese. The efficiency of identifying an East Asian civilization zone probably outweighs the drawbacks, but the label is clearly an oversimplification. We can view Russia as a partial heir to a Byzantine/East European tradition that distinguishes it from Western Europe; thus, we have two major civilization zones in Europe: the West and the East-Central East.

In the postclassical period, a number of regional kingdoms emerged in Southeast Asia. At the same time, this region received significant cultural and commercial influence from other sources, notably, India. Indian traders sometimes brought Hinduism into this region, and the spread of Buddhism from India was even more striking. From India also came inspiration for regional writing systems. Chinese influence is seen here, particularly in the form of increasing trade activity from the time of the Song dynasty onward. By the end of the postclassical period, Islam had gained the greatest religious success in many parts of this region. This pattern of varying outside influences combined with local traditions sets up a different model in Southeast Asia from that seen in Japan and Russia.

Western Europe did not have the same needs that Japan and Russia did from its influences, but West European leaders saw clear advantages in imitating certain aspects of the Byzantine Empire and the Arab world. Western Europe used these contacts to regain knowledge of classical learning that had been preserved by the Byzantines and Arabs. From the Muslims and the Byzantines, Western Europeans also copied a variety of technologies and benefited from Arab advances in medicine, mathematics, and other fields.

The Arab philosophical debate over the boundaries between faith and reason was transmitted to Europe, where it was applied to Christian interests in rationalism. The Gothic arch—that quintessential artistic symbol of postclassical Western Europe—was, in part, adapted from the characteristic Islamic arch. Western Europe borrowed from Islamic innovations in commercial law, identifying principles that could transcend political boundaries and protect merchants regardless of specific location. Whether acknowledged or not, the Western European debt to Islamic and Byzantine examples was considerable. The fact that this period was one of extensive imitation is an important addition to our understanding of postclassical Western Europe.

The imitation process raises one final question for the period itself and carries some interesting implications for more contemporary situations. In all four cases, cultural forms and styles, along with technologies, seem to have been particularly eagerly sought. Why is this so?

One fact that prompts this question is the lack of success with the imitation of political forms. Japan, Russia, and Western Europe were aware that political models existed that were superior to their own decentralized situations. As Japan began to imitate China, for example, it exhibited a deliberate desire to import the Chinese imperial system. For almost a century, the Chinese example was incorporated into Japanese political activity, but the effort failed because Japan could not sustain the same degree of centralization as China. The Japanese solution, during the bulk of the postclassical period, would be a form of feudalism. Russian leaders were aware of Byzantine political examples, but they did not wield the same power and could not establish a tightly organized political system.

New connections were forged between societies in which civilization was a new phenomenon and societies in which the patterns were better established.

The Western Europeans had a chance to establish a more centralized political structure under Charlemagne in the early-9th century. Charlemagne's realm extended to northern Italy, very northern Spain, France, the Low Countries, and parts of western Germany. Charlemagne, however, lacked the resources and, possibly, the experience to set up an independent bureaucracy. Charlemagne ended up reinforcing Western European feudalism.

We see here societies that are capable of imitating models to speed up artistic, literary, and cultural development, but are the imitators inherently less able to use political examples? Is a period of cultural gestation necessary before a society can imitate another society's political achievements, and if so, does this characteristic still apply in the world today? We have a number of instances today in which societies seek or are told to seek political inspiration from countries that have different political experience. Are such models particularly difficult to follow, or is the political delay we have noted confined to the postclassical period?

The postclassical period saw a great deal of deliberate imitation and a substantial degree of success in this arena. Connections were forged between societies that were new to the civilization phenomenon and those in which civilization patterns were better established, but these connections never completely erased issues of definition between such civilizations as Russia and Byzantium or Japan and China.

In three of the major cases—Japan, Russia, and Western Europe—the societies involved were on the peripheries of the most sophisticated patterns available during the postclassical period. These three societies would use this period of imitation as gestation for a later, stronger, emergence in world history. ■

Suggested Reading

Charles Freeman, *The Closing of the Western Mind: The Rise of Faith and the Fall of Reason.*

David R. Knechtges and Eugene Vance, eds., *Rhetoric and the Discourses of Power in Court Culture: China, Europe, and Japan.*

Nicholas Riasanovsky and Mark Steinberg, *A History of Russia*, 7th ed.

Questions to Consider

1. Why was so much attention devoted to imitating cultural building blocks and artistic and intellectual forms? How does this compare to processes of imitation today?

2. How did Western Europe's imitation process differ from that of Japan or Russia? Were the differences significant?

Western Civilization in World Context
Lecture 15

> The great Indian leader Gandhi—according to the story, at least—was once asked what he thought about Western civilization. He replied, "I think it would be a very good idea." He presumably was questioning, at the time when he was in a struggle with the British, whether the West was civilized.

Western civilization is arguably a more elusive concept than Chinese, Indian, or Middle Eastern civilization. World history, including the comparative approach, raises interesting issues about identifying Western civilization. The postclassical period allows some of these issues to be sorted out, though the process must begin earlier. The tradition of teaching Western civilization reflected several factors: an imperialist-style belief that the West was possibly the only superior civilization; a concomitant concern, born in the ashes of World War I, that the West was falling apart and needed historical shoring up; and a belief on the American side that emphasis on Western values would help integrate a diverse and suspect pool of immigrants.

Thus Western civilization advocates tended to argue that there was a straight line from the earliest great civilizations to the glories of Western Europe later on. Beginning Western civilization with the river valleys, however, raises two questions: First, what was Western about them? And second, how can we account for the greater legacy of the river valleys to later East European and Middle Eastern societies? Should the Western tradition, then, be traced to the classical Mediterranean? This is certainly possible, though there is much about classical Greece and Rome that does not seem particularly Western; the societies themselves (particularly Greece) tended to look eastward.

The first indisputably Western civilization, in fact, emerged in Western Europe during the postclassical period. It had several features that have survived, and it was, as we have seen, a somewhat underdeveloped borrower during the period. But by the later postclassical period, it was possible to identify a Western civilization and compare it with the Asian and African cases.

It is impossible to teach a full Western civilization program in the framework of world history; thus we will look at a more subtle issue involving the Western civilization tradition, namely, the extent to which the West is sometimes viewed almost unanalytically.

We can begin by situating the West among certain other definitional issues previously evoked. It is harder to pinpoint the origins and characteristics of Western tradition than of Chinese or Indian tradition.

One problem in looking at the classical Mediterranean tradition as the origin of the West is the extent to which this tradition fed not only the West but also a number of other societies, including Eastern Europe and the Arab world. This fact makes it difficult to extract exactly what is Western in this tradition. The same thing holds true in the great debate between rationalism and faith.

Another problem in overemphasizing the classical origins of a Western tradition involves how much of the classical tradition did not survive or, at least, did not survive in any direct sense. Classical Greek and Roman attitudes toward homosexuality did not form part of the West's later tradition. The democratic strand in the classical Mediterranean was not predominant, and its link to the revival of democratic ideas in the late-17th and 18th centuries is almost nonexistent. We cannot deny, however, that some aspects of the classical past would survive or be revived to form part of the Western self-perception.

Some common aspects of Christianity raise questions about the boundary lines between the West and the larger Christian world, but defining the West as a civilization is not as problematic as defining Japanese or Russian civilizations. We're skating here between two levels of definitional difficulty: the West seems harder to define as a civilization tradition than India or China but easier than certain cases where imitation was even more rampant.

An argument can be made that the postclassical period is where we find some distinctive features that become demonstrably and durably Western. The West was defined by Roman Catholic Christianity, where we find some of its organizational features. The Western tradition of Christianity posited a certain degree of separation between the religious tradition and political structures. Although these distinctions could be blurred, this separation is different from the East European Christian tradition and Islam.

The Western form of feudalism ultimately developed a pre-modern parliamentary tradition. Feudalism was taken to mean that rulers had some obligation to consult with their vassals in making certain crucial decisions, particularly where taxation and budgets were involved. This Western parliamentary tradition appears in Spain, England, and elsewhere by the 13th century and becomes a durable part of Western political structures.

A third feature involves the political power and independence of Western merchants in the postclassical period. The West was not the world's commercial or capitalist leader in the postclassical period, but Western merchants were less constrained by political regulation in interregional trade than was the case elsewhere.

Some authorities on Western Europe in this period have argued that through Christianity, the West developed a sense of the superiority of man over nature that resulted in a special interest in new technologies. Scholars have posed an interesting argument about a distinctive kind of Western family structure that would emerge at the end of the postclassical period and intensify in the centuries thereafter. In this structure, ordinary people married fairly late, replacing extended family traditions with nuclear families.

Are we well served in looking at the postclassical period as a formative one for Western civilization? This period is one in which some classical traditions were incorporated or reused and in which some activities developed as a result of the imitation of other societies. In this period, a set of specifically Western themes emerged in a few crucial areas of political, social, and economic relationships that we can trace from this point onward.

Another aspect of the task of positioning the West in the postclassical period involves, again, the process of imitation. In relation to other societies operating in the postclassical period, the West was rather backward. Western civilization did not command great respect in the Islamic world.

Many Western leaders in various spheres of activity felt this gap as well, which is why they proved such eager imitators. Westerners frequently traveled to Muslim Spain, the Byzantine Empire, and Egypt and were filled with awe at the standards of living they encountered. This gap also explains why the Crusades had their primary impact on the West: the revelation of the difference in living standards between the West and the Middle East spurred new levels of Western trade and consumption. The Crusades also highlighted the paradox of the West's firm conviction that it possessed essential religious truth but, in virtually every other respect, was a somewhat backward society.

From the Middle East, we've seen that the West eagerly borrowed a number of technological and cultural devices, but opportunities also opened up in new Western connections with China.

The West participated actively in postclassical trade, and this trade increased as Western society gained vigor, particularly from about 900 or 1000 C.E. onward. But as the West entered increasingly into interregional trade patterns, it did so with two distinct disadvantages. Some of the goods that were most sought after in the West inevitably depended on Islamic middlemen. Western traders had to go to Egypt or the eastern Mediterranean to obtain goods from India, China, or the Middle East, which meant an additional price to pay to a series of middlemen. These middlemen were emissaries of a religion that was viewed as heretical and inferior to Christianity.

The larger problem, however, was a balance-of-payments issue. The West wanted spices, silks, and other goods from Asia, but Western manufacturing offered almost nothing to world trade. When Vasco da Gama reached India, he brought with him Western textiles and crude metal products that the Indians were not interested in because their products were much better. Europe existed in the postclassical world as an increasingly eager but disadvantaged participant in larger Afro-Eurasian patterns. One response was to become enthusiastic imitators of technological and other developments.

Toward the end of the postclassical period, certain occurrences began to create new opportunities for the West. Regional competitors encountered new difficulties. The Byzantine Empire declined, and Arab political unities were shattered. These developments presented new opportunities to borrow technologies from other societies that could help the West overcome its disadvantages. From China, at the end of the postclassical period, the West adopted a number of technologies, including the compass and explosive powder. The printing press, initially invented in Korea and China, was brought to Western Europe and put to use by a variety of inventors.

Western political capacities began to improve in the last centuries of the postclassical era with the emergence of feudal monarchies. Frequent military conflict also spurred the West's interest in technological developments that had military applications. Textbooks in Western civilization routinely assume that changes in the West in the postclassical centuries were the crucial determinants of later Western activity in the world as a whole. World historians, however, take a slightly more cautious view: new opportunities for imitation and the results in terms of a new world role came first and inspired. ■

Suggested Reading

Christopher Dyer, *An Age of Transition? Economy and Society in England in the Later Middle Ages*.

David Landes, *Revolution in Time: Clocks in the Making of the Modern World*.

Peter N. Stearns, *Western Civilization in World History*.

Questions to Consider

1. How do the arguments for a Greco-Roman origin for Western civilization compare to those for a postclassical origin?

2. What were the major strengths and weaknesses of Western civilization compared to other major civilizations at the end of the postclassical period?

The Mongol Years
Lecture 16

We're talking in this session about an extraordinary period in world history that covers much of the 13th and 14th centuries, 100–150 years. This is a period that [is] known now as the Mongol era or interlude in world history.

W orld history during this period was dominated by the conquests of the Mongols. The Mongols, a nomadic people from Central Asia, began a conquest of China early in the 13th century. Within a few decades, an interlocking network of Mongol empires, or *khanates*, stretched from China in the east to western Russia, embracing a significant part of the Middle East and pressing into Southeast Asia, while organizing much of the Mongol heartland in Central Asia.

Mongols were regarded as bloodthirsty conquerors; they could make cruel examples of civilian populations who tried to hold out against their attacks. But this bad press also reflected the resentments of conquered peoples such as the Russians and Chinese. World history has rehabilitated the Mongols significantly. Once their rule was established, they could prove tolerant and even enlightened; they certainly did not press subject peoples to abandon existing cultures or local institutions.

More important, the Mongol network greatly accelerated travel and contacts between Asia and Europe, to the primary advantage of the latter. It was under the Mongols that such travelers as Marco Polo brought back information about China and specific access to Chinese technologies, including printing and explosive powder. The Mongol period was short-lived—beginning to fade by the later-14th century—but its impact, particularly in technology exchange, continued to affect world history.

This is the context that prompted *The Economist*, in 1999, to name Chinggis (Genghis) Khan the most important historical figure of the then-closing millennium in world history. *The Economist*, a respectable British periodical, named Chinggis (Genghis) Khan the man of the millennium. This was largely a tribute to Chinggis as the first in a succession of Mongol rulers who would administer their conquests reasonably wisely and would use conquest deliberately to accelerate contact among different peoples. It is true that the Mongols could be cruel, killing urban civilians to ensure that others would yield more quickly to their forces. Nonetheless, the dominant revisionist picture seems valid.

The Mongol invasion of China was the last in a series of eruptions from the nomadic territories of Central Asia that had earlier seen such groups as the Indo-Europeans and Huns pour out. Probably some combination of population pressure in a fairly fragile nomadic economy, political rivalries, and divisions in China itself prompted the Mongols to eye the rich society to their east. The Mongols had long been one of several border people harassing the Chinese and pressing into Chinese territory during the Song dynasty.

When I took history, if the Mongols were mentioned at all, it was with a grimace and an apology because they were bloodthirsty barbarians who killed a lot of people to no purpose whatsoever.

Early in the 13th century, Chinggis Khan conquered a good bit of China. The conquest was completed in ensuing decades, so that Chinggis's grandson, Kublai Khan, became ruler of China. This Mongol rule, known as the Yuan dynasty, would last for most of the next century. Once in power, the Mongols made use of the Chinese government system and bureaucracy, along with Confucian values. Although they disapproved of many aspects of Chinese culture, they were generally tolerant. Mongol rule in China brought clear economic benefits, expanding both manufacturing and trade opportunities. In addition to Chinese bureaucrats, the Mongols used a variety of foreign administrators in a deliberate attempt to open up the society to a wider set of influences.

The Mongol conquest soon branched out from China. In the eastern part of the Middle East, the Mongols conquered Baghdad and overthrew the last Arab caliphate. A Mongol khanate was established in the eastern Middle East which held sway for several decades. Mongol khanates also fanned out in Central Asia, aiding in the first coherent political organization of that region.

The other great conquest of the Mongols involved Russia toward the end of the 13th century. In Russia, rulers were having increasing difficulties with restive nobles. The resulting Mongol sweep across European Russia exempted very few territories but spared Western Europe.

Mongol efforts also pressed into Southeast Asia at key points. By the late-13th century, the block of territory held by interlocking Mongol khanates was without precedent in world history.

The results of these invasions were significant, with some durable elements. Overland travel from west to east became increasingly easy. Popes began to send Christian emissaries to the Mongols quite early, both to persuade the invaders to stay out of Western Europe and Catholic territory and to convert some peoples in the Mongol realms. Western merchants took advantage of the safe passage granted by khans into Mongol territory. We also know of some trips by European Jews, artists, and entertainers. This openness amplified exchanges of knowledge that would gradually begin to close the traditional technology gap between East Asia and Western Europe.

Accelerated contact in this period also had a downside. It was in the Mongol period that the Black Death began in China and spread quickly to the Middle East and Europe. One-quarter to one-third of the population of Western Europe and the Middle East succumbed to the plague. And the advantages of access to new technology may have outweighed the drawbacks of this level of mortality in Western Europe.

Mongol rule began to decline in the latter part of the 14th century. The Mongols were unsuccessful in two efforts at invading Japan by sea, suggesting some limits to their capacity for expansion. The Chinese began to organize more effectively against Mongol rule, ousted the Mongols in the latter part of the 14th century, and quickly established the Ming dynasty.

Mongol rule in Russia ended later. Early in the 15th century, local Russian rulers increasingly asserted their independence. By 1450, an autonomous

Russian area was established in the Moscow region, which then became the center of Russia.

The expulsion of the Mongols from China and Russia led to reactions that indicated the distaste that these peoples felt for Mongol control. The Chinese would become preoccupied with creating systems to prevent the return of invaders like the Mongols—including the reconstruction of the Great Wall of China. The Russian reaction was to undertake a steady series of conquests, initially designed to push the Mongols farther back but ultimately becoming a durable Russian commitment to expansionism. The end of the Mongol period for world history meant a return to increasing political barriers; the opportunities for overland travel between Europe and China receded for a considerable period of time.

The Great Wall of China.

The Mongol period should be viewed as something of a rebalancing among major societies in Europe and Asia. The Chinese hostility toward outsiders deepened, and defensive barriers were created to prevent future invasion. The Mongols had also confirmed China's importance in world manufacturing. Russians turned from a regional people to an increasingly aggressive and expansionist people. This would be a major theme of the next period in world history and continues to some extent even today.

The Japanese, having faced two Mongol invasions and been spared in one case by a typhoon that destroyed the Mongol fleet, began to think of themselves as superior to China. This sense of Japanese isolation would be an interesting factor in world history in the succeeding period.

Aside from borderline clashes, Western Europe did not experience the cost or anxiety of direct Mongol invasion; instead, it received the benefit of unusually free contact with Asia. The Europeans saw the advantages that new

93

kinds of weaponry could bring to a highly militaristic society. The Europeans would make use of printing in ways that would have deep implications for their culture and bureaucracy. The Europeans, in other words, were the leading beneficiaries from this Mongol era.

Sub-Saharan Africa experienced no particular impact from the Mongol conquests, but at the same time it had no stimulus to learn from new technological opportunities. This was a null case, in other words, that would contrast interestingly with the experience of Western Europe.

The decline of the Mongol system could have overwhelmed the pattern of intensifying interregional contacts that we have so vigorously emphasized for the postclassical period, but this system was so successful in its larger sense that it readily survived the Mongols. The question at the end of the 14th century was not whether world contacts would recede, but rather what system, with what routes and under whose sponsorship, would replace the Mongol system?

> **The decline of the Mongol system could have overwhelmed the pattern of intensifying interregional contacts that we have so vigorously emphasized for the postclassical period. It certainly diverted contact opportunities.**

The Mongol era briefly replaced and extended the system created earlier by the Arabs, but it was not the last gasp of global interconnections. That chapter was about to reopen in new ways in the 15th century. ∎

Suggested Reading

Thomas Allsen, *Culture and Conquest in Mongol Eurasia.*

Gerard Chaliand, *Nomadic Empires: From Mongolia to the Danube.*

Jack Weatherford, *Genghis Khan and the Making of the Modern World.*

Questions to Consider

1. Is the shift in evaluation of the Mongols historically appropriate, or does it suggest a troubling change in contemporary values toward more tolerance for bloodthirsty conquest?

2. In Afro-Eurasia overall, which societies benefited, which societies were disadvantaged, and which societies were unaffected by the Mongol conquests?

Civilizations in the Americas and in Africa
Lecture 17

Civilizations in the Americas began before the postclassical period. Indeed, for fairly obvious reasons, since the Americas were not directly connected to Asia, Europe, and Africa, the periodization of the postclassical period is somewhat artificially imposed on the Americas.

Important developments occurred in the Americas and Africa during the postclassical period, and of course, they abundantly illustrate the theme of the expanding geography of civilization as a form of human organization. The Americas offer a particular challenge because of the lack of connection to the rest of the world. One scholar, annoyed at the problems world historians have with pre-Colombian America, has written a book called *1491: Revelations of America before Columbus*.

The facts remain, however, that vital American developments do not cleanly fit the larger patterns of the period and that, because of later devastation, the heritage of the Americas for subsequent history was limited as well. Africa is a different case, complicated mainly by a long tradition of historical neglect. African kingdoms and trading patterns in the postclassical period were deeply connected to the larger world network of the time. Differences from the Americas are thus clear; the really interesting comparisons involve such places as Western Europe.

Early civilizations emerged in Central America, and suggestions of early civilization are found a bit later in the Andes. The postclassical period itself captures the final flowering of Mayan civilization in Central America, the later decline of the Mayans, and the emergence of a mixed Mayan-Toltec society in parts of Central America.

Also in Central America, the Aztec Empire arose in the mid-14th century. The Aztecs were immigrants from the north into central Mexico and other parts of Central America. The Aztec empire would flourish during much of the 15th century. The postclassical period captures the development of further civilization activities in the Andes, particularly the emergence of the Inca

Empire from about 1400 onward—stretching over a long swathe of territory along the Pacific Coast of what is now Latin America.

Developments in American civilizations in the postclassical period emphasized continued improvements in agriculture. American societies were based on the cultivation of several key crops, including corn and potatoes. The emphasis on agriculture and the careful organization of cultivation produced amazing population concentrations and impressive cities by the 14th and 15th centuries. Trading activities were also extensive, with networks running throughout Central America.

Interesting cultural forms arose in the American civilizations, seen in artistic representations of fierce gods and goddesses, as well as impressive scientific developments.

Scholars debate the question of how to place American patterns into a larger world framework in this pre-Colombian, postclassical age. Charles Mann recently published *1491: Revelations of America before Columbus*, in which he takes world historians to task for failing to do full justice to the richness and detail of pre-1492 American history. These societies had no effective contact with other parts of the world. Although this isolation did not hamper their development before or during the postclassical period, it did create vulnerabilities once contact was established.

American societies lacked certain technologies, such as the use of metal for weaponry or tools and the use of wheels on devices other than toys. The Americas lacked a rich mix of animals that were candidates for domestication. Because they had no routine contact with other parts of the world, peoples in the Americas were vulnerable to diseases that had been acclimatized in Afro-Eurasia, notably, smallpox and the measles. Once contact was established, American societies would suffer dreadfully.

The divide between the Americas before contact and the Americas after contact is crucial; given the vulnerabilities in the Americas in technology, animal domestication, and disease immunity, developments there would be superseded by European and African patterns. The Americas may have had occasional contacts from other civilizations, but these contacts were not sufficient to counteract this region's isolation from the world network.

The Americas offer some comparisons with other early civilizations. Some scholars have noted a vague similarity between the Inca Empire, with its emphasis on a divine ruler, and ancient Egypt. This can be contrasted with a slightly more Mesopotamian civilization, such as Central America.

Although American society was overwhelmed after 1492, it was not obliterated. Important traces of earlier artistic impulses, polytheistic religion, and aspects of local village organization and agricultural practices would survive, particularly in Central America and the Andes. It is important to recognize that the legacy here was limited. The problem of integrating the American patterns of the postclassical period with larger patterns remains considerable.

In contrast to the Americas, Africa fits quite well into the larger patterns of the postclassical period, including its involvement with the world network. Agriculture and ironworking were introduced early in Africa, and the spread of these developments south of the Sahara proceeded relatively steadily before and during the postclassical period. In a process known as the *great Bantu migrations*, peoples originally located in west-central Africa moved southward and eastward, bringing with them agriculture, ironworking, and new kinds of political organization. The spread of the Bantus was a major development in terms of connections among African language groups.

Early civilization activities in sub-Saharan Africa focused in the upper Nile area in some connection to developments in Egypt. Significant states and cultures developed in Kush and Aksum, followed by the establishment of an Ethiopian state. These activities took place in connection with patterns in the Middle East and the eastern Mediterranean, which is one reason that Ethiopia received early influences from Judaism and Christianity.

In the postclassical period itself, two centers of activity developed in Africa. The Swahili belt stretched along the Indian Ocean coast in mixed Arab-African communities. This region encompassed an active set of trading societies and developed a written language and political organizations of the city-state type.

Larger kingdoms featuring powerful rulers emerged in sub-Saharan West Africa. Sometimes called *Sudanic* after the Arab word for "black," these kingdoms experienced increasing trade activity, including activity that would connect West Africa across the Sahara to North Africa and the Middle East.

In fitting sub-Saharan African patterns into the larger network of world history, we need to explore a few issues. It is possible to suggest a few characteristic African themes, particularly in the Sudanic kingdoms of West Africa. These civilizations were vigorously polytheistic and used polytheism to emphasize the close connections between human activities and the forces and features of nature. These civilizations tended to emphasize the divinity of major rulers. These civilizations focused on extended families and the connections between individuals in this life and ancestors. These fairly general features can be used to provide at least some baseline for discussions of African characteristics that cut across states and even larger regions.

There is a complicated relationship between African developments before and during the postclassical period and the great religious and philosophical systems that developed elsewhere. African development featured the manipulation of great traditions, particularly those derived from Islam and Christianity. In both the Sudanic kingdoms and the Swahili belt, African developments were powerfully influenced by Islam. Outside the Swahili belt, however, Islam did not, at this early point, become a mass religion.

Sub-Saharan African history in the postclassical period should be viewed in much the same framework that we used for Japan, Russia, Southeast Asia, and Western Europe. Sub-Saharan Africa is another civilization in active contact with the most prosperous centers of the world, benefiting from trade with these centers and imitating some of their features but also maintaining a separate sphere of existence.

One African historian has proposed a close comparison between developments in sub-Saharan Africa during the postclassical period and those in Western Europe. Using a rough date of 1250 C.E., he argues that the similarities in these societies are quite striking. Both civilizations contained significant kingdoms, larger in Africa and loosely organized. Although Africa did not develop literal feudalism, its rule had some overtones of the jockeying necessary in European feudal monarchies. And both civilizations developed new commercial centers and saw increased activity linking commerce to the Mediterranean and Middle East. Merchant activities were important to both civilizations as well, not only in their own right but also in stimulating other economic developments and political activity.

If one looks at the same two societies 200 years later, however, the comparative situation changes markedly. European societies, particularly Spain and Portugal, were actively engaged in exploratory trips down the African coast and were experiencing rapid changes in political and cultural systems. African kingdoms did not exhibit the same kind of outreach and commitment to major change as Western Europe, largely because they did not face the same need for outreach as Western Europe. The year 1450 finds the fates of these two societies beginning to diverge. ∎

Suggested Reading

Philip Curtin, et al., *African History from Earliest Times to Independence*, 2nd ed.

Charles C. Mann, *1491: New Revelations of the Americas before Columbus*.

Michael Moseley, *The Incas and Their Ancestors: The Archeology of Peru*.

Robert Sharer, *The Ancient Maya*.

Questions to Consider

1. How important is pre-Colombian American history in world history? What's the best case for relatively substantial attention?

2. If West Africa compares favorably with Western Europe around 1250, in terms of international role, trade, and even politics, how and why does the comparison around 1450 begin to look so different?

The World in 1450

Lecture 18

We're going to be talking about 1450 in terms of significant changes taking shape in a number of different regions of the world, not just one.

A number of took place by the middle of the 15th century, Many of these crucial changes would set the stage for the next period in world history. Several of the developments were conditioned by the decline of the Arabs and the receding of the Mongol empires. The most familiar, undeniably important change involved the increasing explorations by Europeans down the African coast; this pattern, however, must be put into a world historical perspective. China made a number of crucial decisions in this period also, extending and then ending a fascinating series of expeditions. Russia, by 1450, was casting off Mongol rule but was also deeply affected by the death throes of the Byzantine Empire. Change in the Middle East highlighted the rise of the Ottoman Turks, a development with implications for Europe and Russia as well. Quite coincidentally, changes in the Americas prepared for later shifts in the global mix.

Almost all world historians agree that around 1450 or 1500 a significant break occurred in world history. By 1450, the great era of Arab politics and merchant activity had passed, as had the Mongol era. Given the demise of these two great systems and the continued importance of interregional economic and cultural contacts, what kind of system would replace these previous frameworks?

Specific developments in the first half of the 15th century focused on China. With the expulsion of the Mongols from China at the end of the 14th century, the Ming dynasty came to power. Like many new dynasties, it was vigorous, benefiting from an expanding economy and interested in new political statements and a degree of territorial expansion.

Beginning in 1405, under the Ming, the Chinese mounted a series of huge expeditions that took troops, goods, and political and cultural representatives from the Pacific Coast of China through Southeast Asia to East Asia, South Asia, West Asia, and the Indian Ocean coast of Africa. These expeditions were likely mounted to extend the Chinese custom of seeking tribute from neighboring contacts. For 30 years, these expeditions provided the most striking interregional contacts operating during the 15th century as a whole.

The expeditions were successful in bringing Chinese connections to Indonesia and other parts of Southeast Asia; in establishing a new Chinese presence in India; and in establishing links directly with the Middle East, particularly the Persian Gulf region, and with the states of East Africa. The expeditions were an important assertion of economic strength, building on the established position of Chinese manufacturing that had begun in the Song dynasty and had been extended under the Mongol Yuan dynasty.

Forbidden City, an imperial palace built early in the Qing dynasty.

In 1433, the expeditions were ended by imperial decision. There may have been a certain traditionalist bureaucratic suspicion of these costly expeditions on the grounds that they overemphasized naval activities and commercial groups. A new Ming emperor wanted to establish policies that would be different from those of his predecessor. It is also possible that although the expeditions had resulted in considerable tribute, the crude economic calculation—in terms of short-run cost benefits—argued for termination.

The new representative of the dynasty further believed that investment monies should go to two other important projects. One project was a new Ming capital in Beijing. Another project was the reconstruction of the Great Wall of China (to keep the Mongols at bay). The end of the Chinese expeditions did not end China's economic role in world trade, nor did it isolate China from the rest of the world. It did, however, signal an end to the brief flurry of Chinese initiative into the rest of the world.

A second center of developments around 1450 involved the Middle East and southeast Europe. The decline of Arab rule in these regions left openings for the immigration of new peoples from Central Asia, particularly the Osmanli Turks or Ottoman Turks, who began to appear around 1450.

The Ottoman Turks were fervent Muslims, heavily influenced by Sufism. As they migrated into the area, they seized territories from Arab states and focused on attacking the Byzantine Empire. A major player during the postclassical period, the Byzantine Empire had been declining for some decades before 1450; this decline made the empire a prime target for this new series of interlopers. The Turks laid siege to Constantinople, and in 1453 the city fell and was renamed Istanbul; this fall is one of the great events in world history. For the Middle East, the fall represented a clear step in the establishment of the Ottoman Empire, which would provide a new source of political and military power to a region that had been fragmented for almost two centuries.

The fall of Constantinople also represented a new opportunity for the Turks and Islam to move into the Balkans and southeastern Europe. Even before the fall, the Turks had seized territories in parts of modern-day Greece; thus the change for southeastern Europe was in many ways just as great as the impending change for parts of the Middle East. The Byzantine Empire had been the model for Russian development, and the collapse of Constantinople represented both a terrifying challenge to the Russian sense of identity and gave Russia a new sense of itself as heir to the mission of the old empire.

The fall of Constantinople was a symbolic and real challenge to other parts of Europe, including Western Europe. West Europeans, particularly Italians, had treated Constantinople scornfully in the last days of the Byzantine Empire. West Europeans ignored appeals from later Byzantine emperors for assistance against the assailing Turks, but when the city fell, Europeans had to face the fact that a bastion of Christianity had been removed in favor of a new and fairly potent Islamic presence. In conjunction with these developments, Russian political rulers began to fully cast off Mongol rule in the early-

15th century. By 1450, a steadily expansionist Russian state was forming around Moscow, and the fall of Byzantium served as an additional spur.

Not every place in the world changed or changed significantly in 1450. Africa experienced basic continuity, despite political shifts and changes in trading patterns. The rise of the kingdom of Songhai was an important development in the Sudanic region. The year 1450 was not a striking point in Japanese development even though some adjustment took place. Developments in India were not marked by any dramatic shifts around 1450. The more dramatic changes would come 50 or 70 years later with a new series of Islamic invasions into India.

We also find significant developments in the Americas. By 1450, both the Aztecs and the Incas were beginning to encounter new challenges to their rule. Quite independent of other events, then, the political structures of the late postclassical period in the Americas were beginning to unravel. This would facilitate European entry after 1492.

The final series of developments occurred in new forms of European outreach. Beginning as early as the 13th century, individual merchants and rulers had shown some interest in breaking the confines of European geography and its focus on the Mediterranean as an artery of trade. Farther to the north, Scandinavians had crossed the Atlantic and reached North America, then retreated to more interesting and durable settlements in Greenland and Iceland.

By the early-15th century, patterns of exploration down the African coast were extended. This exploration was sponsored by the king of Portugal, newly freed from Muslim control, and by rulers in Spain. The explorations pushed steadily down the African coast, partly in search of gold. The larger framework, however, was the recognition that Europe faced difficulties in postclassical interregional relationships. The Europeans had developed a taste for Asian goods but not the capacity to pay for these goods; by seeking new sources of gold and other opportunities, the Europeans were trying to remedy a clear problem in their interregional outreach.

Europeans also wondered if they could find a direct connection with Asia around the African coast to avoid Islamic middlemen and cultural challenges. This interest in finding solutions to the cultural and economic problems of dependence on Islamic merchants was further galvanized by the fall of Constantinople and the new potential for Muslim organization in the eastern Mediterranean.

The conventional textbooks on West European history offer a somewhat different background to these new expeditions. By 1450, European political capacity was beginning to improve. The feudal monarchies in England, France, and increasingly Spain and Portugal had achieved a bit more central control over their territories. They also had somewhat greater capacity to guide trade policy and mount significant exploratory expeditions.

European Christianity, not a new force, may have been given a new lease on life in terms of missionary spirit by the expulsion of the Muslims from the Iberian Peninsula. Spanish and, to a lesser degree, Portuguese Catholic leaders played prominent roles in the explorations that began to take shape in the 15th century.

We also need to acknowledge new attitudes developing in the Renaissance, first in Italy and, by 1450, spreading more widely. The Renaissance brought new attention to this-worldly activities and suggested new confidence in the potential of individual achievement. Nonetheless, the world history picture continues to be more complicated than a focus on just the West allows. Key problems remained in terms of world position, including the issue of Islamic intermediaries and the need to compensate for Islamic control in the eastern Mediterranean.

The key point, in concluding about 1450, is to emphasize the variety of developments that were occurring and the number of different places that were involved. There's no tidy pattern.

As the expeditions unfolded in 1450 and afterward, they reveal a few other points that bring us back to motivations. The expeditions failed to find massive troves of new wealth, although they did find some new territories. Europeans began to take over island groups in the southern Atlantic, such as the Azores and the Canaries. The native populations of these islands were extremely vulnerable to some of the common diseases brought by the Europeans, resulting in rapid depopulation. This was, at once, a useful development for the Europeans—local resistance was minimal—and a challenge because of the obvious need to find additional sources of labor.

The solution adopted was to raid the northwest African mainland, where slavery was well established, for sources of labor. The Europeans began to import African slaves into these island groups with the purpose of establishing sugar cultivation. This policy was perfectly understandable in terms of European interest: The Europeans had an economic problem, and growing sugar—rather than importing it from Asia—was at least a partial remedy. Nonetheless, this policy of economic exploitation raised some interesting questions about the nature of the European role in the world as Europeans gained new levels of power.

Once the Europeans succeeded in rounding the southern tip of Africa and reaching Asia directly, they still had a balance-of-payments problem. When Vasco da Gama returned to India for a second time after 1500, he brought a solution to this problem in the form of guns. Da Gama deliberately slaughtered a number of Indian officials to induce the rest of the population to trade, even though the Europeans did not yet have much to offer in the exchange.

Moving forward from 1450, a variety of developments occurred in a number of different places. Both the Chinese expeditions and their curtailment set the stage for European initiatives that would form a new framework for interregional trade. Developments in the Middle East, the arrival of the Turks, the fall of one of the great Christian empires, and the beginning of new assertions by Russians also need to be factored into the world picture.

The end of the postclassical period saw the gradual emergence of a new system of interregional trade that would be immensely important, but it also saw power and cultural shifts in other regions. It also set the stage for a complex pattern of development in world history's next period. ∎

Suggested Reading

Felipe Fernandez-Armesto, *Millennium*.

David Northrup, *Africa's Discovery of Europe, 1450–1850*.

Kenneth Pomeranz, *The Great Divergence: China, Europe, and the Making of the Modern World Economy*.

Questions to Consider

1. Should China have continued its overseas expeditions, and how much difference would this have made in world history later on?

2. How much should the standard explanations of the "rise of the West" beginning in the 15th century be modified in light of Europe's problems and the ongoing strengths of other societies? Where does the European Renaissance fit in the larger panorama of world history?

The Early Modern Period, 1450–1750
Lecture 19

Today, we'll be talking about the early modern period in world history, a period that runs roughly 1450–1750, the next period after the great postclassical millennium.

The most important development in this new period of world history involved the rise of international trade and the redefinition of this trade to include the entire globe for the first time. Western Europe was a key agent in much of this change, including the new contacts with the Americas and, at the end of the period, with Pacific Oceania and Australia.

The conventional emphasis for the period, in terms of a fascination with growing European strength and changes within Europe itself, is accurate but should not overshadow the broader patterns of change. European dominance of the Americas and its new influence in Africa are qualified by a much more complicated relationship with most of Asia.

A final theme for the period—what historians often call the age of *gunpowder empires*—calls attention not only to the emergence of Europe's overseas colonies but also to the rise of several new land-based agglomerations in Asia. The early modern period thus focuses on new patterns of trade and new exchanges, along with a new spurt of empire formation from several sources. Strong elements of this new global economic system persist today. Interestingly, the period is not defined by any overall patterns of cultural change, despite significant developments in particular regions.

In contrast to the classical and postclassical periods (lasting 1,500 and 1,000 years, respectively), the early modern period is relatively short (300 years). One explanation for this shorter time span may be that the pace of change became more rapid.

As we get closer to the present we have more abundant records. We also tend to spend more time on periods that are closer to the present because, inevitably, they have more influence on current patterns of activity.

Some historians would argue that 1500 is a better date for the start of the early modern period. By 1500, it was clear that the Europeans would introduce significant changes in the Americas. By 1500, the Ottoman Empire had expanded from southwestern Europe and the northeastern Middle East to include portions of North Africa, especially Egypt. The end of the period, 1750, is a date of convenience meant to indicate the coming changes brought on by European industrialization.

The early modern period is where many world history educational programs go awry, focusing on European power after 1450 and the glories of change in the West. This view distorts and over-simplifies the continued complexity of the world as a whole. We must recognize that the power of Western Europe did increase and that the nature of the West itself was significantly transformed. That said, Europe did not run the world in 1750: many societies, continued to act independently of Europe, and important developments occurred that had very little to do with Europe.

In establishing a new period in history, we must show that the previously predominant themes have lost some force. The postclassical period was defined by expansion in the geographical range, the number of civilizations, the impact of the world religions, and the establishment of a world network connecting different parts of Africa, Asia, and Europe. Because the main contours of the civilization zones were fairly well established, expansion was no longer a dominating principle.

For the world as a whole, the religious map was fairly well established. The world network was still an operative concept but was transformed by of the inclusion of the Americas. The earlier network was an intense interrelationship among different societies in what we might call the Old World; the new world economy is global and even more intense.

What, then, are the new themes? The most important developments in the early modern period are the intensification of interregional trade connections and the inclusion of the Americas (and later Pacific Oceania). Other new themes include the new power relationship of the West in the world, the biological exchanges that resulted from European and African contact with the Americas, and the "explosion" of gunpowder empires.

Carlo Cipolla sums up the expansion of Europe in the title of his book, *Guns, Sails, and Empires*. By the 15th century, Europeans had adapted Chinese explosive powder for use in guns, particularly cannons. The technology for casting church bells was transferred to casting bronze and iron cannons. Sails came from adaptations of Arab shipping, and Europeans learned how to make more effective oceangoing vessels, which proved to be particularly successful in navigating the waters of the Atlantic and then the Pacific; at the same time there was an increasing use of navigational devices such as the compass.

Guns and sails in this period took Europeans to islands and coastal regions where they could establish oceangoing contact and use their sea-based cannons to intimidate and threaten. Europeans seized port cities in West Africa and occasionally East Africa, some ports in India, island groups in what is now Indonesia, territory in Taiwan, and the Philippines. With rare exceptions, the interior of Africa and Asia would remain immune to European conquest at this point.

In the Americas, Europeans had the added advantage of metal tools and technologies, horses, and military organization that, in some instances, was superior to that of the Native American peoples. The Europeans also had the "advantage" of disease. Up to 80 or 85 percent of the total Native American population died off from disease within two centuries. This cleared the way for European conquest as no other development could.

With regard to the European weapons and naval advantages, we might well ask why no other society in the early modern period chose to rival the Europeans in this game. Several other societies had metalworking traditions, shipbuilding capabilities, as well as experience in interregional activity, but chose not to imitate the European patterns of expansion. The Chinese had no use for such expansion primarily because it did not serve the purposes of Chinese society itself. The case is similar in Japan. In the 16th century, the Japanese were especially interested in new types of European weapons but at the end of the century they cut off European contacts, partly because Catholic control in the Philippines was viewed as a threat and European weapons endangered the system of feudalism.

The sense that European patterns were not relevant to the goals of key societies motivated a distinctive stance toward European technology. Europeans, in turn, viewed themselves as having a technological edge over the new societies they came in contact with and began to judge other societies mainly by the state of their technology.

Another key development in this period involved what historians routinely call the *Colombian exchange*. This term refers to the fact that biological products moved from the Americas to the rest of the world and vice versa, an exchange that was almost entirely disastrous for the Americas. Biological exchange meant that Old World domesticated animals were brought to the Americas, as were Old World food products. Unfortunately, the main biological import to the Americas was disease. At first, the impact was accidental, though by the 18th and 19th centuries, Europeans deliberately introduced diseases into Native American populations in order to clear them out. The Colombian exchange for other parts of the world was arguably beneficial; American food products began to spread widely to other areas, helping to sustain and even augment populations.

African involvement in the Colombian exchange was complicated. New World foods, particularly corn, spread widely to Africa and helped sustain population development. But another biological exchange took the form of people themselves moving to the Americas. Beginning in the 16th century, 8–12 million Africans would be seized in the Atlantic slave trade and taken to the Americas. This level of displacement had serious consequences for Africa—particularly West Africa—because a disproportionate number of the slaves were young males at a prime age for reproduction. The most vigorous impact of the Colombian exchange had ended by the early-18th century. People became more resistant to disease in the Americas, and the bulk of the population was now of mixed European and Native American heritage.

The early modern period is also known as the age of gunpowder empires. The Europeans, led by the Spanish and Portuguese and followed by the Dutch, British, and French, established their overseas empires in the Americas and in parts of Asia and Africa.

Equally important was the establishment of land-based gunpowder empires in Asia. The Ottoman Turks, for example, had used gunpowder and cannon in their siege of Constantinople and established their empire partly based on this technology. The Mughal Empire in India was also organized by invaders using new weaponry. The Safavid Empire in Persia and the Russian Empire were based in part on gunpowder.

The new empires that arose in Eastern Europe and much of Asia were quite different in orientation from the more commercially minded overseas empires but equally important because they maintained sway over a significant landmass and dynamic economies. Even in China, the Qing dynasty, launched in the 17th century by Manchurians, was partly a gunpowder empire.

The early modern era is not a distinct period with regard to gender relationships, although we can see some changes. The arrival of Europeans in the Americas had implications for American gender relations because European values and expectations differed greatly from Native American traditions. In withdrawing men from Africa, the slave trade increased the importance of polygamy to provide family arrangements for the remaining women. There is no blanket pattern, however, that allows us to use the early modern period for purposes of gender discrimination.

Along with the rise of the West comes the establishment of really significant political units in other parts of the world that would long overshadow Western politics per se.

In the same way, culture in the early modern period reveals changes in specific cases but no blanket pattern. The importation of European religion, artistic styles, and some science to the Americas was a major change in American cultural history. European culture would also change with, for example, the rise of science and the division of West European Christendom. In the world as a whole in the early modern period, however, there is no overall cultural dynamic: individual societies, such as Japan or China, would indulge new opportunities for contact to a degree but not at the expense of substantial cultural differentiation.

Let us close by reviewing the main themes of the early modern period. The rise of Europe was accompanied by the establishment of significant political units in other parts of the world that would long overshadow Western politics. The biological exchange that resulted from the inclusion of the Americas in the world network prompted various reactions. Many societies had to make decisions about how to handle new contacts with the West, including whether they would make use of new foods. They also had to make decisions about the impact of new imperial structures, land-based as well as sea-based.

The central theme in this period was the intensification of economic relationships, which now also included the Americas and, at the end of the period, parts of the Pacific. One interpretation of this period argues that the West managed to position itself as a transmitter of American goods, and this transmission served as the engine of the world economy with much more diverse benefits and implications than we usually think of when we look at the rise of the West alone. ■

Suggested Reading

Michael Adas, *Machines as the Measure of Men: Science, Technology, and Ideologies of Western Dominance.*

Carlo Cipolla, *Guns, Sails, and Empires: Technological Innovation and the Early Phases of European Expansion, 1400–1700.*

Noel Perrin, *Giving Up the Gun: Japan's Reversion to the Sword.*

Jeffrey Pilcher, *Food in World History.*

Questions to Consider

1. How did growing Western dominance compare with previous Middle Eastern dominance of world trade? Were Western policies harsher or more benign in their impacts on other societies?

2. Why did the rise of the West not generate wider interest in Western cultural forms during the early modern period?

Lecture 20: The World Economy, 1450–1750

The World Economy, 1450–1750
Lecture 20

> In introducing the early modern period of world history in our last
> session, I emphasized—I frankly think it's pretty obvious—that the big
> deal development underlying all the others was the intensification of
> world economic relationships and the inclusion of the Americas into
> those relationships.

In the early modern period, world trade increased, becoming literally
global and seeing an increasingly powerful role for the West. Above all,
trade became more important to many societies, helping to shape not
only economic life but political and social systems as well. With the growing
importance of trade in such products as slaves, sugar, silver, guns, and elite
craft items, a number of societies began to develop elaborate relationships of
superiority and dependence.

Western Europe became the superior player: It had strong governments and
a flexible wage labor system, and it emphasized manufactured products such
as guns or luxury furnishings, that could earn top money in world trade. The
West carried the trade in its ships and commercial companies, other sources
of profit. On the other hand, peripheral societies exported cheap foods and
raw materials, using coercive labor to cut costs (and to respond to labor
shortages), relying on merchant companies and ships from the European
core, and importing more expensive items.

Weak governments followed from the lack of an ample tax base, the
interference of the West, and the desire of landlords to regulate their own labor
forces. Wealth flowed from the periphery to the Western core. Latin America,
the Caribbean, and the North American South were the classic peripheries,
but West Africa, with its slave trade, had peripheral characteristics. By the
18th century, grain-exporting regions such as Poland, which relied on serf
labor, were becoming peripheries also. The biggest problem with the world
economy approach, for the early modern period, involves the continuing
success of Asian economies, headed by China. We will take this complexity
into account as we discuss the world economy.

When we discussed the world network in the postclassical period, we mentioned that it was capable of affecting basic manufacturing patterns, as in China, for example. When we look at the early modern period, we see the same kind of intensification operating at a higher level in a set of different economies.

Immanuel Wallerstein, an American sociologist, developed *world economy theory* to explain this intensification; the theory is a useful device for exploring relationships in the early modern period and even in the present day. In addition to illustrating general points about intensification, world economy theory has three advantages.

It clarifies systematic inequalities in international economic relationships that emerged in the early modern period and, thus, helps explain why societies otherwise as different as Latin America and Poland can be viewed through something of the same lens. It deals with relationships between export and import activities within societies, economic position in the world economy, and political structures and labor systems. It helps to explain why certain patterns endure for so long and why they are hard to eliminate. We should note, however, that world economy theory has been widely criticized for omitting certain factors (such as culture and technology) and for oversimplifying some points. The theory also has difficulty in dealing with change and does not do justice to the complexity of patterns in Asia.

Wallerstein introduces four key concepts, three of which we will discuss in this lecture. He identifies core and peripheral societies—the "winners" and "losers" in the early modern world economy. Because not all societies were fully enmeshed in the world economy at this point, Wallerstein also brings in external societies, in which the economy is not primarily dependent on global relationships. Wallerstein argues that these economic relationships—particularly the crucial duo of core/periphery—are born with the early modern period. Although elements of these relationships existed in the postclassical period, they become more rigorous in the period we are discussing.

Examples of core societies include Spain and Portugal in the initial phases of the early modern period and Britain, France, and Holland by the 17th century. A core society makes profits from the world economy by exporting finished goods, organizing the trading companies that direct world commerce, and building and running the ships that carry trade. In the long term, the core society profits from the world economy because of its capacity to control activities and facilities in these three categories.

Economic advantage, however, is closely linked to political advantage. In Wallerstein's view, core societies not only have profitable economic relationships internationally, but they also have fairly strong states. As a society profits from the international economy, tax revenues increase, enabling the society to fund a more elaborate system of government. With a strong government backed by a strong military, a core society can intervene in international situations in ways that will help position its merchants advantageously. Wallerstein also argues that core societies increasingly adopt wage labor systems, using wages to motivate workers and to locate workers where manufacturing opportunities exist.

Peripheral societies are the mirror image of core societies. Peripheral societies have dependent economies through which they import expensive products primarily from core societies and export raw, unprocessed goods. Trade in peripheral societies is carried by merchants from core societies and depends heavily on ships from core economies. Obviously, peripheral societies tend to lose money in international economic exchange. They are just as fully engaged in trade as core societies, but their engagement involves systematic disadvantages.

Peripheral societies have weak governments because they do not have the tax revenues to strengthen government. The core societies have a stake in keeping these governments weak so that their own merchants and interventions will not encounter resistance. Peripheral economies (at least in the early modern period) do not rely primarily on wage labor but on forced or coercive labor, slavery, or harsh serfdom.

These economic, political, and social system or labor system relationships are easily uncovered in the early modern period. The core societies initially were Spain and Portugal, although ultimately, their positions slipped. In the end, the great core societies were those in much of the European northwest— France, Holland, Britain, and others. These societies spawned large trading companies that organized trade and sent out ships. These societies also experienced a significant and steady increase in manufacturing, including both craft manufacturing and domestic or home production.

In using Wallerstein's theory, we need to guard against oversimplification. For example, although France and Britain were both core societies, France had a much stronger government and military than Britain in the early modern period.

The classic peripheral society, of course, was Latin America. Latin America produced sugar, silver, wood products, and other goods that were mostly sent elsewhere for processing. In its colonial period, Latin America experienced quite weak governments. Latin American economies featured, essentially, versions of serfdom, the *encomienda* and *hacienda* systems, in which laborers were forced either to work certain days or to turn over certain percentages of their products.

Wallerstein notes that by the 18th century, peripheries were developing in parts of Eastern Europe, particularly Poland; there, amid harsh serfdom conditions, emphasis was increasingly placed on producing grain for sale in Western markets. In this trade, we see Polish reliance on the export of relatively cheap products, carried in Western ships, in patterns organized by Western merchant companies.

West Africa can also be seen as a peripheral economy if we argue that slaves constitute unprocessed goods. African slave systems developed through a combination of African merchant and political organization, occasionally with some direct European intervention. Slaves were then sold to European traders and transported by European ships and commercial companies. In return, African merchants and political figures received processed goods from the core societies.

In looking at the peripheral societies, again, we need to be aware of oversimplification and some other rough points in categorization. For example, although West Africa was a peripheral society, its governments were much stronger than those of Latin America and much more capable of regulating European activity. As European intervention increased in India and what is now Indonesia, economies there developed some peripheral characteristics, although they did not shift entirely to a peripheral status.

The British colonies in North America also present problems of categorization. The South, with its concentration on the production of sugar and other goods for sale to Europe, clearly was a periphery. The middle colonies and New England, however, did not fit easily into Wallerstein's scheme. These areas had a significant local merchant class, engaged in some manufacturing, and ran some shipping, but they were not yet core economies.

The key issue in Wallerstein's theory, however, is Asia. Wallerstein does not deal with Asia in great detail in his treatment of the early modern period, but the implications of his work suggest that Asia must be viewed largely as an external economy, that is, the Asian economy was not sufficiently involved in world trade to be affected by world trade dimensions. This position feeds and is fed by misperceptions about Asia's economic role in the world in this period, including its degree of isolation and disdain for commerce. If we dispel these notions, the idea of externality must be largely dispelled as well.

Japan had the one clear external Asian economy by the 17th century. Around 1600, the Japanese cut off elaborate contacts with the West; without question, Japan's economy was not a significant participant in world trade patterns in the 17th and 18th centuries. Because Japan recognized the utility of maintaining some outlet to the wider world, however, the Japanese allowed the Dutch to trade near the port of Nagasaki. Externality was not complete, but Japan fits the external category fairly well in this period. Indeed, the early modern period saw considerable development of commercial operations in Japan, although not as a result of external economic relations.

For the Middle East, India, and particularly China, however, externality simply does not apply. China received the largest amount of New World silver of any society in the 16th–18th centuries, largely as the European solution to its old balance-of-payments problem for Chinese exports. This flood of silver into China had significant impact. In the 17th century, for example, the Chinese government decided that all taxes must be paid in silver currency. This requirement almost certainly resulted in increased inequality for peasants. China could not possibly earn this much New World silver and be regarded as an external economy, but it is not exactly core either because Chinese merchants and ships did not go out into the world beyond Southeast Asia. China was a manufacturing powerhouse but not, for foreign trade purposes, a commercial powerhouse; China had a strong government and traded actively with Southeast Asia, but on a global basis it did not operate as a core society.

> **It is possible to fall out of the core— Spain and Portugal did—if you don't make full use of your economic superiority … .**

Some of the same points apply to India, at least until the 18th century. India was the second largest recipient of New World silver because the Indians also had a variety of goods that Europeans desired. India, however, had little need for European goods during the early modern period. By the 18th century, with increased foreign intervention in India, its position shifted into a more dependent category, but for most of the early modern period both India and the Middle East had some advantage in trade with Europeans.

A modified view of the early modern world economy system makes sense. With regard to Latin America, Africa, and some parts of Eastern Europe, European economic dominance is real; it is a source of new profits for the West and new patterns of economic and political activity for the peripheral societies. Nonetheless, this is not yet a world system, and it must be modified to account for not only the decline of Spain and Portugal but the new position of India. Wallerstein's picture is further complicated by such factors as population shortages and cultural attitudes. Properly adjusted, Wallerstein's theory explains why different societies fell into systematic patterns of inequality in the international marketplace in the early modern period and why this system tended to be so persistent. It is possible to fall out of the core, as Spain and Portugal did, but it is much more difficult to climb out of the periphery. ∎

Suggested Reading

David Eltis, et al., eds., *Slavery in the Development of the Americas*.

Kenneth Pomeranz, *The Great Divergence: China, Europe, and the Making of the Modern World Economy*.

Immanuel Wallerstein, *The Modern World-System II: Mercantilism and the Consolidation of the European World-Economy, 1600–1750*.

Questions to Consider

1. Why and in what ways was much of Asia long resistant to the core/periphery relationships in the world economy?

2. Do the core and periphery models adequately capture relationships among economic, political, and social forms during the early modern period?

Lecture 20: The World Economy, 1450–1750

Transformations in Western Europe
Lecture 21

It's no secret that the early modern centuries constituted an exceptionally busy time for Western Europe—many changes and significant movements.

Partly because of its growing world role and rising earnings from international trade, Western Europe changed greatly in the three centuries after 1450. Many of the items on a list of key developments are quite familiar: the Renaissance, including the Northern Renaissance; the Protestant and Catholic Reformations; the price revolution of the 16th century (prompted by the import of increasing amounts of silver and promoting further commercial expansion); the rise of absolutism (but also the advent of parliamentary monarchies in Britain and Holland); the Scientific Revolution; and the Enlightenment.

These developments did not all neatly mesh, and other interesting episodes suggested some of the tensions involved with uneven and sometimes contradictory change—the witchcraft craze of the 17th century is a leading case in point. From a world history standpoint, there are two major issues: First, with all due credit to the growing importance of the West, it would be misleading to linger too long over the details of activities in a single society. Second, these changes must be placed in a world history context—compared with developments elsewhere and assessed for their greater impact.

The focus of this lecture, then, is on the big changes in the West and their larger implications for world history. This focus, in turn, calls for attention to growing commercialization in the economy, which paralleled the larger international role; the growth of state functions and the emergence of the nation state; and a series of changes in both formal and popular culture, many of them revolving around the rise of science.

World history does not afford us the opportunity to spend as much time on these developments as we might in a Western civilization approach. How can we make this range of developments in Western Europe manageable enough to fit into a world history pattern?

In this lecture, we will take "a big changes approach," looking at significant shifts in Western Europe between 1450 and 1750. This approach does not do justice to all the individual movements and currents in Western Europe but is necessary for understanding the bigger picture. We will also look briefly at the global implications of these changes. We will evaluate the big changes in the West in terms of their placement among existing global standards.

Big changes in the West in the early modern period fall into four categories. First is the increasing place of the West in world trade and, to a lesser extent, in world power politics. From world trade, the West gained access to new ideas and perspectives and new levels of wealth and commercial opportunity. Although we will focus on the other three big developments in the West, this repositioning in the world was a fundamental change in and of itself. The other three big developments involved an increasing commercialization of the West European economy, increasing governmental efficiency and rationalization, and fundamental shifts in cultural outlook.

The first of the three is commercialization. During the 16th, 17th, and 18th centuries, more Europeans became involved in the commercial economy, producing at least some goods for sale on the market. In the 17th century, southern French peasants and landlords began producing wine for sale to other regions, thus involving themselves in importing food for consumption. Villages began to specialize in certain kinds of production. In both agriculture and manufacturing, ordinary people, as well as merchants and landlords, began to produce more for the market and to adopt an explicit set of market motivations and practices.

This meant a growing importance for the merchant class of Western Europe, which expanded and gained wealth from both international and domestic trade. The expansion of domestic manufacturing in Western Europe was also important. Under this system, rural people devoted more effort to producing goods for sale to merchants in nearby cities.

Commercialization was accompanied by a growing gap between the large numbers of people who owned property and the propertyless or near propertyless workers. European class structure shifted away from the community-based relationships that had predominated in the postclassical centuries. This change was accompanied by a new and harsher attitude toward poverty, even as early as the late-16th century. This commercialization of the European economy falls under the heading of a catch-up development. It brought Europe to economic levels that had previously been achieved in such places as China and other parts of Asia.

By the 18th century, developments began to press beyond the catch-up level. The expansion of domestic manufacturing and the introduction of new technologies (such as the flying shuttle in weaving) pushed the European economy beyond levels that had been achieved in other societies. Another 18th-century development—recently uncovered—is the beginning of modern consumerism in Western Europe, predating the Industrial Revolution.

The second category of development is politics. Until the 17th century, European politics can still broadly be described in terms of the earlier emphasis on feudalism. But by the 17th century, though feudal remnants lingered, European states were beginning to develop a new range of activities and a sense of rationalization.

Central governments now began to send out increasing numbers of bureaucrats to the provinces to ensure that central edicts were enforced uniformly throughout the realm and to monitor local conditions. At this point, national boundaries began to matter. New functions included such activities as cultural intervention. In the 17th century, the French monarchy, for example, established an institution to monitor and regularize the French language; and in this same period, European states began to set up prisons.

Along with the expansion of function came rationalization, an increasingly self-conscious effort to think through how government activities were organized. The military serves as a prime example: in the 17th century, many European armies began to acquire uniforms, define officer grades, formalize training for officers, organize hospitals and logistical systems, and establish pensions. Most of these developments were catch-up activities, that is, European governments were now beginning to do things that political systems in several other societies had already done, although, again, with particular European emphases.

By the 17th and 18th centuries, however, we see an innovative twist—the clear beginnings of the idea of a nation state, a state in which a shared culture and tradition would coexist with the state itself. The nation state concept was a fundamental innovation on the world scene that would have a wide impact beyond Europe as well as within it.

The third category of development is culture. The advent of printing in Europe opened up massive opportunities for Europeans to have contact with the written word. Literacy advanced systematically, and by the 18th century Western Europe had the highest literacy rates of any large society in the world. The Protestant Reformation, despite some effective Catholic response, shattered the unity of Western Christianity and led to internal conflicts and tensions. In the long run it tended to reduce religious commitment in Europe and promote some idea of religious toleration.

During the Scientific Revolution of the 17th century, the range of scientific discovery and the increasing sense on the part of many intellectuals that the key to truth lay in science (not faith or tradition) was a fundamental change that no other scientific endeavor in other societies matched. If we combine science with printing and growing literacy rates, we could argue that of the three areas we have emphasized—commercialization, political change, and culture—it is culture that makes Western Europe stand out from other societies.

The European package—the Western model, if you will—was increasingly complicated, and this would affect responses to Western activities in the wider world, as well.

The other intriguing aspect of cultural change in early modern Europe was the degree to which it penetrated into relatively prosaic activities and into the attitudes of relatively ordinary people. Between about 1600 and 1700, people had vastly different responses to ordinary situations, such as losing a valued object, naming a child, or embarking on marriage. Fundamental shifts in Western culture yielded impressive and varied expressions at the level of popular beliefs and practices, affecting the sense of the individual, the sense of family and community, and attitudes toward risk and nature.

Western Europe, despite all the exciting things happening there, was not the only place in the world. Many regions continued to ignore developments in the West, and some areas, by coincidence, saw a few developments that were not unlike those occurring in the West.

Nonetheless, the changes that occurred in the West in the early modern centuries have three final implications. The big changes we have seen—governments taking on new roles, new attitudes toward nature, and even new attitudes toward children—almost guaranteed that additional changes would occur in the West. Of course, the increasing pace of commercialization set the fundamental framework here. These changes would color European reactions to other societies. Europeans would think of other places as uncivilized because they did not measure up to Europe's new standards. The developments that occurred in the West set a challenging target for other societies. The complexity of the Western model would affect responses to Western activities in the wider world as well. ∎

Suggested Reading

Robert Dear, *Revolutionizing the Sciences: European Knowledge and Its Ambitions, 1500–1700.*

Mary Hartman, *The Household and the Making of History: A Subversive View of the Western Past.*

Ulinka Rublack, *Reformation Europe.*

Charles Tilly, *Big Structures, Large Processes, Huge Comparisons.*

1. How did religious change in Western Europe, notably the rise of Protestantism and the Catholic response, help explain the longer-term changes in commerce, politics, and popular culture?

2. Compared to other major agricultural civilizations by the 18th century, such as China or the Middle East, what was unusual and what was fairly standard about Western institutions and culture?

The Rise of Russia
Lecture 22

The early modern centuries saw what is incontestably a significant rise of Russia in world affairs. It was also a period in which Russian political and cultural patterns changed significantly, as well.

Russia poses a bit of a problem for world historians. Is it a civilization all its own or part of a slightly larger East European civilization? Should it be handled, as is commonly the case in European history texts, as part of Europe, though not a leading part? And how important is Russia? Developments in the early modern period, crucial in Russian history per se, suggest the need to treat Russia separately but with a clear asterisk; they also suggest the importance of Russian expansion on the world history stage. Early modern Russia warrants attention as an unusually durable example of the phenomenon of gunpowder empires; as a society increasingly influential in Middle Eastern and Asian, as well as European, history; and as a first instance of selective Westernization, an example of a pattern that would resound more widely in world history later on, providing, among other things, a comparative benchmark.

The early modern centuries saw a significant rise of Russia in world affairs, along with important changes in Russian political and cultural patterns. Categorizing Russia is a bit of a problem for world historians. In these lectures, we have defined Russia and, possibly, a larger Eastern European zone as a distinct civilization, although new relationships Russia developed with the West in the early modern period blur this distinction somewhat. An East European zone existed beyond Russia's borders—sharing with Russia, in some cases, commitment to Orthodox Christianity and to some common agricultural systems.

The primary Russian theme in this period was territorial expansion. Between 1450 and 1750, Russian territory expanded steadily in several directions, not yet reaching its current dimensions but, without question, creating a substantial gunpowder empire. One factor that pushed Russia to expansion was the desire to drive the Mongols further away. Russia was also driven by the idea of itself as the heir to the Byzantine Empire. Along with this notion was some sense of a religious mission. Russia frequently insisted that it had a role to play in the Middle East in defense of Christianity, especially Orthodox Christianity. As the early modern period progressed, the Russian state and individual groups, such as the Cossacks, also developed a direct stake in expansion. Expansion was one of the ways in which the tsars could justify their rule; other groups sought new opportunities to obtain land.

Expansion took several directions. The most important expansion was southward into Central Asia and to the borders of the Ottoman Empire. Here, Russia began to influence world affairs in fundamental ways. By the 17th and 18th centuries, Russian-Ottoman conflict increasingly moved to the advantage of the Russians. Russia was involved in pushing the Ottoman Empire back, gaining new territories to the south and the southeast in the process. Russian expansion also eliminated Central Asia and its nomadic groups as an independent factor in Eurasian affairs. Russian expansion, along with Chinese and Ottoman expansion, increasingly placed most of Central Asia under the control of an organized state. Russian expansion began to produce a Muslim minority in Russia. Although Russia cast itself as a European state, the tsar presented himself as a ruler who operated in a Muslim tradition.

The second direction of Russian expansion was westward, when Russia began to move into Ukraine and other territories that brought it directly into East-Central European affairs. By the end of the 17th century, Russia played a role in military and diplomatic interactions with such countries as Sweden, Prussia, and Austria-Hungary. After about 1750, Russia would assume a more general role in European diplomacy. This push westward brought new minorities into Russian rule, including Jews and German ethnic minorities.

The third direction of Russian expansion was eastward, across the Ural Mountains into Siberia and, ultimately, even beyond. By the 18th century, this move brought Russia into direct contact with China. The mid-18th-century Amur River Treaty established a border between China and Russia that indicated the extent to which Russia was now a minor player in East Asian affairs.

During the 18th century, Russia pressed beyond East Asia into Alaska, and Russian explorers moved south from Alaska into present-day northern California. Russian trading expeditions even reached the northernmost island of Hawaii.

By 1750, Russia had one of the largest landmasses under single rule that had ever existed. This expansion established Russia as a multinational society at the same time that Western Europe was emphasizing the nation state. This multinational quality would be both a strength of and a challenge to Russia from this point onward. This expansion also established Russia as a frontier society, particularly in the East but also in parts of Central Asia.

Two devices were used in the early modern period to hold the Russian territory together. The first device was the strong assertion of the power of the central state and its ruler, the tsar, but state authority was often hollow. The second device was, essentially, an agreement between the state and the landlord class.

Both big landlords and gentry-level landlords were given increasing political and economic powers to run local courts, administer justice, punish criminals, levy taxes, and require labor service from serfs. This decentralization into estate-based management gave Russia the opportunity to establish at least some political stability even in its huge new territories.

Once in a while, this agreement between the tsar and his nobles broke down and trouble ensued. For the most part, however, the agreement held steady because both parties had a stake in preserving this system.

In the later-17th century, Russia embarked on another important pattern of change: Westernization. Peter the Great decided that to maintain Russia's military mission and to further Russia's goals of becoming a European power, significant changes had to occur involving Russia's imitation of patterns then visible in the West.

Westernization reforms under Peter took several directions. One set of changes was what we might call cosmetic. Peter insisted that his nobles trim off their Mongol-like beards and adopt Western dress, rather than Asian.

Western cultural institutions were imported into Russia, notably, the ballet. These various changes added up to a major effort to alter Russia's cultural orientation in significant directions.

The second set of changes involved efforts to improve Russian education, particularly for the upper classes, and scientific work. Under Peter, new scientific academies and universities were established, including the State University of St. Petersburg. All nobles were to receive training in mathematics; they would not be allowed to marry if they did not obtain an educational certificate. The third set of changes was political and fairly straightforward. Peter developed somewhat more specialized bureaucratic services and created a state counsel to oversee bureaucratic activities.

Peter the Great.

Peter instituted significant, though not uniform, military and economic changes. He established a Russian navy, importing Western artisans and advisors to do so. He tried to improve the armament of the Russian army, and reorganized the army into somewhat clearer categories of command along partially Western lines. He also organized the Russian metallurgical industry, taking advantage of Russia's holdings in iron ore to build an economic basis for independent weapons productions and to equip Russia's armies without having to rely on Western imports.

What were the goals of Peter's program of Westernization? The first goal was to enhance the power of the tsar and the state in what was still a fairly ineffective state apparatus. The second goal was to enhance the power of the Russian military so that it could play a role in European affairs and would have an edge in its military conflicts elsewhere, specifically, with the Ottoman Empire.

The third goal was to address what one might call an embarrassment factor with Russia vis-à-vis the West. Peter assumed that interchange between Russia and the West would become more frequent and that, without some changes, Russia would be viewed by Westerners as barbaric and backward. One way to deal with this problem was to make at least upper-class Russia look increasingly Western.

Equally important, however, was what Peter the Great did not Westernize. He did not import Western ideas about constitutional monarchy, the parliamentary tradition, or the division of powers.

Peter was not interested in any significant reforms that affected ordinary Russians. He did not ameliorate the conditions of the serfs, nor did he institute a wage labor economy in Russia. He did not try to bring cultural or educational change to ordinary Russians.

Perhaps most revealing of all, Peter clearly did not want to make Russia a commercial economy in the Western model. If we go back to the terms of the world economy, Peter's goal was to maintain Russia as an external economy, capable of producing what it needed for its own economic operation and for its expanding military activity but not seeking commercial dominance over areas outside of Russia.

Peter the Great's changes … [would] continue to differentiate Russia from the West per se, while connecting it to the West without any question.

The Westernization program was quite real, but ironically enhanced some of Russia's differences with the West. Russia joined Western cultural life, and Peter the Great was obviously eager to further Russia's role as a European diplomatic and military player, but he was not interested in creating a Western society. In confirming or widening the gap between ordinary Russians and the upper classes, Peter created circumstances that were quite different from those of the West and would have different outcomes later.

Peter's changes had at least two unintended consequences that, from this point onward, would inform Russian affairs and continue to differentiate Russia from the West while also connecting it to the West without any question. After Peter's death, Orthodox clergy and some landlords voiced concerns about the implications of Westernization; the result was an ongoing ambivalence about what Russia's relationship with the West should be. Although Peter intended for Russia to remain an external economy, his actions encouraged involvement in the European-dominated economy on terms that were not favorable to Russia. The desire for Western goods pushed Russia into the position of a peripheral economy, emphasizing timber, minerals, and grains in its exports and depending on serf labor.

Westernization probably did help maintain the military strength of the Russian imperial experiment, but it also set in motion other currents that would have further effects on Russia's relationship with the wider world—sometimes fostering new links, particularly with the West, but sometimes creating new tensions as well. ■

Suggested Reading

Lindsey Hughes, *Peter the Great and the West: New Perspectives.*

Michael Khodarkovsky, *Russia's Steppe Frontier: The Making of a Colonial Empire, 1500–1800.*

Richard Stites, *Serfdom, Society and the Arts in Imperial Russia: The Pleasure and the Power.*

Questions to Consider

1. What kind of relationship to the world economy did Peter the Great seek: a European-style core position, a peripheral position, or something else? What position resulted from Russia's version of Westernization over the longer term?

2. Why and how did serfdom become a dominant issue in Russian history?

Asian Empires and a Shogunate
Lecture 23

Our focus in this discussion is on Asian societies during the early modern period. Frankly, it's a presumptuous combination. This is a huge territory with all sorts of different societies that experienced all sorts of different developments during this long period, but a few generalizations are possible ... .

Key changes marked the experience of the leading Asian societies during the early modern centuries, changes that had little to do with developments in the West or Russia. The Asian continent, although involved in the world economy, was long buffered from its worst pressures. The formation of new empires—the Ottoman, the Safavid, and the Mughal—brought significant cultural and political changes. In China, a more familiar dynastic cycle saw the Ming rise and decline, to be replaced by the nation's final dynasty, the Qing. By the 18th century, however, several of the Asian gunpowder empires were faltering.

The Mughal Empire was in serious trouble, though technically it survived into the 19th century. The Ottoman Empire passed its expansionist prime in the 17th century, though it retained great power. The situation in China was more complex, but there were signs of new difficulties by the 18th century. Each imperial pattern had its own dynamic and characteristics, but it is legitimate to ask if there were some shared issues. Finally, Japan, though not an empire, experienced significant change as well, important at the time and for the future.

Contrary to longstanding presumptions, most Asian societies in this period were actively engaged in wider connections in the world, although on different terms from those that operated in the West. We can identify two major developments in Asian societies during the early modern period. The first development was increasing prosperity, at least for some groups, as a result of Asia's participation in production for world markets in exchange for American silver. This participation confirms, among other things, an interest in export-based manufacture in parts of China and an interest in transmission to world markets in India. The second development was the emergence of a series of gunpowder empires in much of the Asian landmass.

The Ottoman Empire began to take shape in the middle of the 15th century and extended its hold over much of southeastern Europe. It developed significant holdings in much of the Middle East, extended its direct control to Egypt, and had some nominal control over other parts of North Africa, though not Morocco. The Mughal Empire emerged in India in the early-16th century as a result of invasions from a force that operated through Afghanistan. The Safavid Empire in Persia was a smaller gunpowder empire that helped revive a sense of Persian identity and presence and maintained significance for a couple of centuries.

China, where the imperial tradition was well established, operated according to a somewhat different rhythm. Much of the early modern period saw the operation of the Ming dynasty, followed by the Qing dynasty, which had some elements of gunpowder empire attached to it, as well. The Qing had been organized by Manchurians coming in from northern China and remained partially outside Chinese culture. This element was not dissimilar to other gunpowder empires, in which an intrusion from outside helped to shape the imperial experience more generally.

These empires had significant accomplishments, although they were not quite as dynamic as those occurring in Western Europe. Asian power began to decline a bit in this period if measured against European power. The longstanding trend in which technological leadership and innovation centered in Asia, particularly East Asia, and tended to move westward began to shift toward greater Western parity and even slight leadership.

The Ottoman Empire brought a number of developments to the Middle East and southeastern Europe, solidifying and highlighting a new Turkish presence in the northern Middle East. But Ottoman administration was never purely Turkish: it incorporated a number of other peoples, including non-Muslims. The Ottoman Empire helped encourage the spread of Islamic belief to parts of southeastern Europe, although Christian groups were, for the most part, tolerated. The Ottoman regime also confirmed a dependent and inferior political status for Arabs. The Ottoman Empire introduced cultural changes into the Middle East: a form of mosque developed that blended Byzantine architectural forms with Muslim needs; Ottoman contributions to literature and art, often in Arabic, were also significant.

Mughal contributions to India were numerous. At its high point, the Mughal Empire encompassed a system of considerable tolerance and a mixture of Hindus and Muslims. They introduced additional cultural richness into the Indian tradition, including Persian and Western artistic influences as well as important individual symbols such as the Taj Mahal. They promoted the possibility of creating larger territorial units in the Indian subcontinent, which would feed directly into Indian unity after the passing of British rule. They also developed administrative and taxation structures that had lasting impact in India. And the Mughals were interested in reforming certain traditional Indian practices, such as the practice of *sati*, though results here were meager.

Hagia Sophia in Istanbul, Turkey.

Developments in Safavid Persia included a revival of a sense of Persian identity. It was under the Safavid Empire, for example, that Farsi was established as the dominant language of the region. Developments in Qing China included economic prosperity and the re-elaboration of the bureaucratic imperial state. Significant population expansion occurred under the very late Ming dynasty and the Qing. During much of the early modern period, Asian empires—largely independent of Western influence in any cultural or political sense—made important achievements that would outlast the empires themselves.

Some of the gunpowder empires began to show signs of wear as early as the late-17th or early-18th centuries. The Safavid Empire began to weaken in the early-18th century, and the Mughal Empire began to weaken even somewhat earlier. If their goal was to preserve Indian vitality and Mughal rule, then later-17th-century Mughal emperors made two mistakes. Several later emperors began to reverse the policy of religious tolerance, clearly favoring Muslims in administration and creating an atmosphere of religious mistrust. The second mistake was overexpansion. The attempt to press Mughal boundaries southward led to significant military expenditure at the expense of the taxation base and the basic economic vitality of India as a whole.

By the 18th century, Mughal hold over India began to fade in favor of local princes, and Indian economic prosperity declined. It was in this context that European powers, ultimately led by the English, began to interfere in Indian affairs. The British East India Company took advantage of Mughal weakness to establish a beachhead on the continent. The later-18th century saw the increasing conversion of much of India to, essentially, a British colony.

The Ottoman Empire presents a different picture. This regime reached a high point in the late-16th and 17th centuries. A last effort at territorial expansion occurred in the 1680s, as Ottoman troops twice attacked Vienna, hoping to press farther into Central Europe. These attacks failed and, from that point onward, the Ottomans suffered territorial setbacks. These setbacks pressed the empires in other ways: It became harder to reward loyal bureaucrats and generals. Many parts of the empire were parceled out among chief administrators who might meld the provinces for personal advantage. Corruption and economic dislocation increased.

Nonetheless, the Ottoman Empire remained healthy well into the 19th century. By the 18th century, sensing Ottoman weakness and undoubtedly exploiting an older prejudice against Islam, European opinion began to hold that Ottoman rule was both sick and weak. This perception would create a reality of its own during the 19th century and affect Europe's relations with the Middle East.

Developments in China were much more complex. In most fundamental respects, the Chinese state and economy remained vigorous up until the 1830s, but there were some modest signs of trouble. Probably by the 18th century, China began to be burdened by overpopulation that would affect larger economic dynamism and growth. At the same time, China ceased being a source of major technological innovation, and cultural creativity lagged. The empire may also have been affected by excessive bureaucratization that made decision-making difficult and communication with the provinces cumbersome.

These empires, particularly China and the Ottoman Empire, did not look to selective developments in the West as a model for certain reforms, as Russia had done. China had been open to modest Western activity in much of the early modern period, but this openness turned sour in the early-18th century. Participation in trade remained vigorous, but there was, if anything, a withdrawal from an interest in contacts of other sorts.

The Ottoman Empire rather systematically avoided the possibility of influential imports from the West. The printing press was banned from the empire until the middle of the 18th century, when it was first allowed only for Christians, not Muslims. This was an obvious attempt by the government to control access to information and ideology. The only Western influence directly incorporated by Ottoman rulers, interestingly enough, was Western doctors, who were called upon to service the Ottoman court. For most of the early modern period, significant achievements were registered in Asia, but these gains were somewhat overshadowed by the greater vigor of developments in the West.

Japan contrasts to some extent with the developments in the gunpowder empires we have seen thus far. The early modern period was a crucial one in Japanese history. After some flirtation with Western contacts, Japanese leaders decided at the end of the 16th century to close off contacts and emphasize internal economic, political, and cultural development.

This period became known as the Tokugawa shogunate, which would last until 1868. Under the shogunate, the ritual apparatus of feudalism was carefully preserved, along with the social privileges of feudal lords. Alongside feudalism was the apparatus of a small but definite central state. The shogunate was the framework for the successful expansion of commercial activity in Japan.

The Japanese turned increasingly to Confucianism during the early modern period. As Confucianism spread, this-worldly concerns began to predominate in Japanese culture, along with new artistic forms that would mark further steps in Japanese cultural identity. Japan also saw an increasing commitment to education, not just for the upper class but for broader bands of society. Over time, Japanese Confucianism encouraged an educational commitment that would position Japan as the second society, after the West, in literacy rates by the early-19th century.

The Japanese population did not grow massively during the 18th century. The fairly extensive use of abortion, among other things, seems to have limited Japanese population growth.

Also important for the future of Japan was the tendency in the 18th century to become slightly more open to outside influences. This interest indicated that the Japanese were aware of developments in the outside world and saw a need to find out what these developments might portend.

The patterns we have discussed in this lecture do not overturn conventional views of Asian history in the early modern period entirely. Relative decline is undeniable, but it must not overwhelm our understanding that important positive developments took place during much of this period.

At the same time, we should note the decline of specific regimes, most notably in Mughal India. But the sense that Asia began to be backward or isolated in this period is simply wrong. World historians, particularly experts on Asia and the world economy, have insisted that we need to redress this impression of Asian economic inferiority and backwardness.

Asia was not simply sitting around waiting for Western control and guidance. This was a series of independent kingdoms capable of significant achievements.

One reason for this insistence is, presumably, that it is better to be accurate than not. Another reason is that our misguided impressions pander to older Western prejudices about Asian characteristics. Asia remained a vital contributor to world history up until at least the 18th century and even into the 19th and would again become a vital contributor by the 20th century. ■

Suggested Reading

Rifa'at Abou-El-Haj, *Formation of the Modern State: The Ottoman Empire, Sixteenth to Eighteenth Centuries*.

Catherine Asher and Cynthia Talbot, *India Before Europe*.

D. E. Mungello, *The Great Encounter of China and the West, 1500–1800*.

Questions to Consider

1. Did the Asian societies make a serious mistake in long ignoring and, in some cases, avoiding Western patterns of change in the early modern period?

2. Why and in what ways was Mughal decline more serious than the issues emerging in other Asian societies by the 18th century?

The Long 19th Century
Lecture 24

In this session, we introduce the next major period in world history, which runs from about 1750–1914. … . This period shades off from the early modern period in several ways—although as I mentioned before, there's no decisive break.

World histories usually mark a new period in the later-18th century, contending that even though not all the themes are entirely new, there is enough change to warrant separate treatment. We look then to a period running from around the 1750s to World War I, which historian Eric Hobsbawm has dubbed "the Long 19th Century." This new period saw the decline or disappearance of most of the earlier land-based empires in favor of a simpler pattern of ascendant European imperialism. Europe's growing world dominance correspondingly redefined the world economy, which for a few decades balanced between a European (and U.S.) core and the peripheralization of almost every other region.

The overwhelming new fact was the steadily growing manufacturing and military might of Europe, soon intensified by the results of the Industrial Revolution. Industrialization displaced much regional manufacturing in favor of European imports and generated changes in military technology that not only increased Europe's superiority on the seas but added ready dominance on land, as well. Around the edges of Europe's industrial dominance, two other themes began to emerge: first, a pattern of selective imitation of certain European developments that might be called the beginnings of modernization, copying elements of technology or education, for example, while retaining distinctive political forms; and second, the emergence of new levels of international connection under Western control that might be called a first stage of contemporary globalization.

Two features of the early modern period, the Colombian exchange and the land-based gunpowder empires, no longer had much impact in world affairs in the Long 19th Century. At the same time, two themes of the early modern period persist in this period.

• The rise of the West, which continued and even accelerated compared to other societies.

• The clearer shape of the world economy.

The two big developments that framed the Long 19ᵗʰ Century are the emergence of the Industrial Revolution and its brief but decisive monopoly by the West. The Industrial Revolution introduced a new economic form as decisively different from agriculture as agriculture was from hunting and gathering. Almost every aspect of life was touched by the Industrial Revolution as it began to take shape, first in Britain, then in other parts of Western Europe and the United States in the late-18ᵗʰ and early-19ᵗʰ centuries. The Long 19ᵗʰ Century is also shaped by the extent to which Western societies monopolized the industrialization process. Ultimately, industrialization was a global phenomenon, but for the Long 19ᵗʰ Century itself, the enhancement of European power by industrialization set a framework to which every society had to react.

Even in its European monopoly, the Industrial Revolution was already, in crucial ways, global. Europeans industrialized in part because they had already learned that an emphasis on producing processed goods was the way to make money in the world economy. Producing processed goods in factories simply enhanced and augmented that advantage. Global relationships had also helped pile up capital in European coffers that was now available for investment in industrial apparatuses.

Industrialization had a global impact almost immediately, for example, in causing the deindustrialization of local industries in such places as India and Latin America. As British, European, and American factories poured out cheap manufactured goods, hundreds of thousands of domestic workers in Venezuela, India, and elsewhere were thrown out of work, forcing crucial economic adjustments in these regions.

Industrialization and European monopoly shaped the period in crucial respects. As Europe industrialized, it enhanced its demands on other parts of the world to produce cheap raw materials and foods and to accept manufactured products. In other words, it increased the extent to which core and peripheral or somewhat peripheral relationships began to predominate, not just in the Atlantic economy but worldwide. Latin America, for example, already a peripheral economy, saw more land and more workers devoted to production for export. Products here (such as silver, sugar, coffee, rubber, and fertilizer) still depended on low cost and yielded a modest profit to the society as a whole. As this relationship between Europe and other parts of the world was extended, the gap between core societies and peripheral societies widened as well.

Africa was now deeply affected by the world economy. The slave trade was abolished in the 19th century, significantly limiting the principal African product in the world economy; yet African attachment to European goods continued, resulting in a scramble to identify other products that might sell in the world market, such as vegetable oil, palm oil, or cotton. These products, not always suitable to the African environment, required larger amounts of cheap labor, such that, ironically, slavery actually expanded in 19th-century Africa itself. Every part of the world was touched by this relationship, either becoming peripheral or expanding peripheral characteristics.

Another consequence of this new pattern was an extension of European or Western military advantage from the seas to the land. Sea-based power was the dominant source of Western military threat in the early modern period, and it remained crucial. However, a series of developments opened up the possibility of land-based military dominance. These innovations included the development of smaller, more mobile field artillery; the invention of the repeating rifle and the possibility of producing it on a mass scale; and the emergence of early forms of the machine gun.

Land-based military advantage was also enhanced by transportation improvements such as steamships and, in a few cases, railroads, along with the telegraph. Finally, the development of new tropical medicines was an aid to Western military interaction in key parts of the world.

The new Western military edge was demonstrated in a series of major crises that quickly turned into larger patterns of economic exploitation.

The first crisis took place in 1798, when Napoleon invaded and conquered Egypt. Although the British soon ousted the French, the ease with which European forces could conquer one of the heartland areas of the Islamic world was not lost on the Egyptians or the Ottomans. The balance between European military authority and Middle Eastern military power had been dramatically altered.

The second crisis was the first Opium War in China in 1839, in which the British insisted that the Chinese accept opium (produced in British territories in India) and open their markets more generally. The Chinese government, weak now but still with some voice, resisted British demands. The result was a conflict in which British and other Western troops easily overcame Chinese forces and pried open the market for opium and for European and Western activities more generally.

The third crisis took place in 1853, when an American fleet under Admiral Perry sailed into Ito Bay in Japan and demanded that the Japanese open their markets to Western goods. This was followed by another American expedition and a British expedition in 1854. The Japanese ultimately decided that they had no choice but to open their markets.

The fourth crisis arose in 1854–1855, as the Russians were poised to seize additional Ottoman territory. Britain and France objected to Russian expansion and engaged Russia in the Crimea. Although the conflict was not easy, the West won again, and the power of industrial production, transportation, and technology applied to military activities made it clear that even Russia was behind.

After these crises, there followed a series of military penetrations from the 1860s onward in Africa, some areas of the Pacific, and elsewhere. There were few parts of the world that Europe tried to enter militarily and failed. In most regions either direct military penetration or the threat of such penetration now reshaped the world to the West's advantage.

The century of imperialism saw a simplification of the world economic patterns we have described previously.

This new framework was an intensification of patterns that had been sketched, to some degree, in the early modern period, with the addition of two or three other components in the Long 19th Century. The early part of the Long 19th Century, in addition to being an age of early industrialization and imperialistic military activity, was also an age of Atlantic revolutions.

Two Crucial Changes in This Simplification

- One, which we have touched on already, was the increasing exploitation of the bulk of the world by core societies, now including the United States.

- The second change was the effective elimination of externality. No major society could stay external because the West, through military pressure or economic cajoling, simply would not allow it.

Beginning in the 1770s, a series of uprisings occurred in various parts of the Atlantic world, North America, Western Europe, and Latin America that would last through 1849. The ideological thrusts of these movements brought important political ideas onto the world stage, although many of the revolutionary ideals sincerely held by Europeans did not fit the relationships that Europe was forging in Asia and Africa. We see a lag between the emergence of revolutionary ideas and truly global impact. In the 20th century, however, reformers would use the ideologies of the revolutionary Atlantic world to spur national independence movements and social revolutions.

Another new global theme was the need for societies to decide how to respond to Western power. Should societies attempt to resist the West? What aspects of Western development could be imitated to regain or preserve some degree of regional independence?

In the aftermath of Napoleon's invasions in Egypt, a new leader there, Muhammad Ali, undertook a path of reform that he hoped would bring industrialization and modern political and economic conditions to Egypt. Unfortunately, Western pressure and the limits of resources in Egypt tended to confine the durable results of Ali's reforms to the production of new cash crops that could serve the world market. Slightly later, the Ottoman Empire undertook reforms, with mixed results. Russia's reforms, beginning with the emancipation of the serfs in 1861, enabled that nation's participation in the industrialization process by the 1890s.

Western power affected different regions differently. Some areas, such as India and, increasingly, Africa, were held as outright colonies. Some areas, such as China, were simply targets of interference. The responses of different regions varied. Even at the crest of European power we must look at world history in terms of interactions and not simply impositions.

A subordinate theme of the Long 19th Century was the tentative emergence of international institutions and arrangements that accompanied industrialization, and the increasingly global qualities of the world economy. Soon after the middle of the 19th century, for example, the Universal Postal Union was formed, as was the International Red Cross. Other international agreements allowed technological developments, such as the laying of undersea cables. Such agreements were Western dominated and, in one sense, a facet of imperialism itself, but they were also preliminary hints of a partial international political structure. International connections were furthered by the development of new transportation arrangements, including the cutting of the Suez and Panama canals. The 1880s saw the emergence of a series of private, international, nongovernmental organizations (NGOs) dealing with such issues as women's rights and white slavery.

> **This is a story of Western dominance. It is a story of Western economic and military controls that are striking, that make this period, at least superficially, unusually simple, but again, it's also brief.**

New patterns of cultural contacts are intriguing at the end of the Long 19th Century. The first sign of the potential for what we would now call a global consumer culture emerged in the final decade of the 19th century with the internationalization of several Western sports, including soccer and American baseball. This seemingly trivial development points to a final facet of the Long 19th Century: beneath the surface of exploitation and imperialism, new kinds of global connections and contacts were emerging.

Some of these were institutional and some were evidence of international cultural interactions that help shape the next period in world history.

Let us close with a note on the brevity of the Long 19th Century. The Long 19th Century is a story of Western dominance, which makes this period, at least superficially, seem unusually simple. The reason we end the period in 1914 is not only because that date marks the beginning of World War I, but also because, as a result of World War I, the easy Western dominance in the world began to come to an end. ■

Suggested Reading

Shigeru Akita, ed., *Gentlemanly Capitalism, Imperialism and Global History*.

Timothy Parsons, *The British Imperial Century, 1815–1914*.

Peter N. Stearns, *The Industrial Revolution in World History* 3rd ed.

Questions to Consider

1. Why was it difficult for non-European societies to match European economic and military achievements during the Long 19th Century? Why was it hard to industrialize?

2. If one compares India to the Ottoman Empire or China, was it more or less advantageous to be a European colony as opposed to a target of European interference during the 19th century?

Abolition of Slavery and Serfdom
Lecture 25

One of the big changes in world history during the Long 19ᵗʰ Century—
actually starting in the late 18ᵗʰ [century] and extending to 1914 and
even beyond—was a process through which formal slavery was
abolished throughout the entire world.

The abolition of slavery was a major change, reflecting a variety of
new forces in world history and unleashing important new patterns.
In some ways, the change was unexpected in a century that saw
growing levels of economic exploitation in many regional economies. Not
surprisingly, the abolition movements have occasioned great debate. New
humanitarian thinking—arguably, the first global human rights movement—
was an undeniable factor, and the response of many societies to this Western-
centered international pressure was interesting in its own right. But changes
in world demography and migration must also be considered—this was not
simply a selfless movement. Assessing the long-term results of this historic
change is correspondingly intriguing and complex.

In charting the end of slavery, we will look at the issue of causation,
particularly in light of slavery's deep roots and the exploitive economic
relationships that dominated other aspects of world history in this period.
We will discuss the process of abolition, which stretched from 1808 into the
20ᵗʰ century. And we will look at the consequences of abolition, which were
messy, diverse, and global.

Arguments against slavery began to take shape at the end of the 18ᵗʰ century.
Two sources for these arguments predominated in such places as England,
the Netherlands, France, Scandinavia, and British North America. One
source encompassed maverick or new Protestant religious groups, such as
Methodists and Quakers. The other source was Enlightenment thinking,
which stressed the fundamental equality of all human beings. Enlightenment
thinkers also put forth the utilitarian argument that slavery was inefficient.

Agitation in antislavery was not a constant force from the late-18th to the early-19th centuries, but periodically, waves of outrage would develop. Petitions against slavery were signed in England and elsewhere. Plays, pamphlets, and literary materials such as *Uncle Tom's Cabin* attempted to educate people about the evils of slavery. Ineffective boycotts against such goods as sugar were planned.

Principles of the French Revolution also argued against slavery. During the 1790s, the Haitian Revolution, a rebellion against both French colonial control and slavery illustrated the capacity of former slaves to rise against the institution and build a new society.

Some historians have identified the innovation in these abolitionist activities as a new kind of humanitarian thinking. The key principle here was that moral concern should extend to distant situations and to people who were different from oneself, even those of different religions. This concern about morality spread to other areas, for example, Russian serfdom.

The pattern of abolition and emancipation was gradual and varied. The French Revolution abolished serfdom permanently in much of Western Europe, and this abolition would extend into central Germany and Austria through the revolutions of 1848. Britain sponsored an abolition of the Atlantic slave trade in 1808 and in such colonies as Jamaica in 1833. The French Revolution of 1848 extended the attack on slavery in the French colonies. In some of the Latin American independence wars in the early-19th century (for example, in Mexico), the abolition of slavery was part of the process of revolt. In the larger slaveholding societies in Latin America, however, emancipation occurred noticeably later. Russia moved against serfdom in 1861. The argument for emancipation here was humanitarian in part, but a more pragmatic motive was involved as well.

The question of why abolition occurred at this time is not easy to answer. The emergence of humanitarian arguments and campaigns played a role in abolitionist movements. The argument that slavery and harsh serfdom were found to be uneconomical at the time is probably incorrect; slavery was still economically effective in producing sugar and cotton. Some scholars have argued that some of the moral fervor devoted to attacks on slavery was designed to distract industrial workers in northern England and elsewhere from their plight.

Another factor that must be considered is the concern about slave revolts or individual acts of defiance. But except in a few instances, as in Haiti, the abolition of slavery did not directly result from slave protests. We should keep in mind the global demographic context in looking for reasons for the demise of slavery. In the 19th century, population rates were on the rise, which meant that alternatives to slavery were now available in terms of cheap sources of labor.

Slavery, of course, did not die a painless death. Slave owners argued fervently to retain the institution, appealing especially to property rights. This argument was used by planters in the American South and Russian landlords. American slave owners and Russian aristocrats argued that slavery was essential for providing guidance and motivation to childlike peoples.

Efforts to resist the tide of abolition lost. Slavery and serfdom were abolished in the Western world and in territories under Western control by the middle of the 19th century. Slavery and serfdom were abolished in Russia and the United States in the 1860s. Lincoln's Emancipation Proclamation was certainly motivated by some sense of the injustice of slavery but also by

President Abraham Lincoln.

world opinion. Abolishing slavery in the secessionist states was a means of conciliating British and French public opinion, which was otherwise slightly inclined to sympathize with the South against the competitive, industrial North.

Slavery was attacked by European imperialists as they moved into Africa. The "white man's burden" argument viewed imperialism as essential to counter the growing use of slavery in the 19th-century African economy. The abolition of slavery extended to parts of Latin America, such as Brazil in 1882. Later in the 19th century and into the early-20th century, antislavery forces began to attack slavery in parts of the Middle East.

By about 1923, the formal legal institution of slavery was effectively ended. The abolition of serfdom was a little less systematic. In the later 1860s, serfdom was abolished in parts of Eastern Europe, such as Romania, in the wake of Russian reforms.

We can divide the consequences of abolition into four categories. The immediate results of emancipation were very different. When slavery was abolished in Jamaica, way stations were established, in which former Jamaican slaves might be bound to apprenticeships for years. After Russian emancipation of the serfs, a formula was designed to give peasants access to land, while preserving the aristocracy. Some have argued that one consequence of the abolition of slavery in the Americas was an increase in racism.

There's really a direct connection between the kind of world opinion that had formed against slavery and more recent organizations, such as Amnesty International … .

Many societies saw efforts to revive conditions that had some similarity to slavery. In Brazil, orphans were brought into the labor force without choice and treated as slaves until they became adults. In the Belgian Congo, African laborers were forced into the mines on pain of physical mutilation. Slave-like conditions might also result from harsh sharecropping systems in which people could work the land only if they agreed to heavy taxation as a result of their tenure. In many factories in Mexico and the United States, conditions of indebtedness were used to tie workers to the factory owners. In more recent times, Asian workers in some U.S.-controlled Pacific Islands were held under threat of deportation.

With slavery abolished in the Americas, labor needs had to be met by immigration. Sources of immigration to Latin America and elsewhere included Southern and Eastern Europe, as well as Asia and India. The moral outrage that had been mobilized against slavery did not end with the institution's abolishment. In the later-19th century, petitions and education campaigns were directed at new evils such as the exploitation of workers in the Belgian Congo or the phenomenon of white slavery. By the end of the 19th century, organizations to mobilize world opinion applied their efforts to other situations of perceived injustice. This consequence was of great importance for the 19th and 20th centuries and is the final legacy of this interesting moment in the history of the world in the Long 19th Century. ∎

Suggested Reading

Seymour Drescher, *The Mighty Experiment: Free Labor versus Slavery in British Emancipation*.

Peter Kolchin, *Unfree Labor: American Slavery and Russian Serfdom*.

Peter N. Stearns, *World Opinion: Origins and Impact on Modern History*.

Questions to Consider

1. Why, in the final analysis, did antislavery rise at this particular point in world history?

2. In terms of world history, how much really changed as a result of the wave of abolitions?

Modernization and Nationalisms
Lecture 26

[This session is] about new divisions in world history during the Long 19th Century, but we're also going to talk a little bit tentatively about some common trends that cut across these divisions. Then … we're going to talk about the spread of nationalism, which was both a common trend and a source of division … .

Developments in the Long 19th Century divided societies around the world in many ways. The deepest division pitted Western Europe and a few other wealthy societies, such as the United States, against most of the rest of the world, where economic conditions were deteriorating. In 1800, for example, the average Mexican had a standard of living two-thirds the level of his U.S. counterpart; in 1900, the ratio stood at one-third as a result of U.S. gains and Mexican losses. But there were other rifts as well. Some regions were held as colonies, the treatment of which varied greatly.

For all the divisions, however, there were also a few common trends as societies attempted to respond to Western pressure and example. With a great deal of caution, some of these trends can be seen as the first signs of a global modernization process. Three areas warrant particular attention: changes in the military, public health, and education. Another common trend, though by definition a complicated one, involved the spread of nationalism. European in origin, nationalism met a variety of needs in most regions of the world, becoming a significant new political force by 1900. Figuring out what nationalism meant and how it could vary, for example, between reformism and conservatism is a crucial analytical task for modern world history.

We have already noted the important division that opened up in the Long 19th Century between industrialized societies and agricultural societies. We can also point to a division between societies held as colonies and those that remained free. While India was held as a colony, China—technically independent—was increasingly subject to European territorial seizures and exploitation.

Even among colonies, however, we find differences. India fared better under imperialism in the Long 19th Century than Africa did. Africa was divided among competing European states in a race to exploit its territories and resources.

Along with differential economic change and differential imperialism came the realization of the need for certain reforms. Some societies realized that aspects of Western development would need to be imitated if they were to gain enough strength to establish or retain independence in a world dominated by European political control and the control of the industrial zone.

Modernization theory, the brainchild of American sociologists in the 1950s, argues that, as societies realize the directions of modern industrial political states, they begin to change a number of aspects of social activity in parallel directions. According to this theory, societies will begin to move in the same basic directions, and the following connections will be seen among developments in intellectual life, family life, and political life:

- Economic modernization means that societies will become or will try to become industrialized.

- Political modernization means that governments will take on new functions, shed older functions, and create larger bureaucracies; the result is the creation of a new kind of state whose operation parallels the modernization of the economy.

- As culture is modernized, science will be emphasized.

- Modernization can even apply to aspects of family life, where it might involve, for example, reduction of the birthrate.

- Modernization theory is widely assumed in certain kinds of scholarship, but it also has severe limitations.

- Critics argue that looking for a single direction in world history in the modern period oversimplifies very complicated patterns, even within single societies.

- The theory also risks denigrating societies that seem to be slow in the modernization process.

- Modernization theory does not apply to many areas of social life: it doesn't predict, for example, trends in religion, crime rates, or the status of women.

- Finally, modernization must be distinguished from mere Westernization.

At the end of the Long 19th Century and in the early-20th century, we find common trends in three broad areas—public health, education, and the military—in virtually every major society in the world. Borrowing from Western sanitary ideas and engineering, many societies realized that governments needed to take responsibility for public health measures, which would result in healthier and more rapidly growing populations—sources of economic and military strength. Modern public health measures were born in Western Europe in the 1830s and 1840s and spread to the United States, Japan, Latin America, and elsewhere. Public health became a concern in the urban sectors of virtually every part of the world by the end of the 19th century, setting the stage for the huge global population increase of the 20th century.

By 1900, virtually every society in the world was also attempting to spread schooling to some sectors of the lower classes and to add technical and scientific subjects to the educational agenda. This might be a massive effort, as in the West or Japan, where by the 1890s virtually every child of appropriate age was in school. Much more gradually, colonial authorities in India and Africa began to allow some access to education, sometimes assisted by missionary efforts. China would expand its attention to student life by the 1890s, sending students to learn from such societies as Japan, the United States, and Western Europe.

Recognizing the now more ominous power position of the West, societies looked to improve military technology and copy Western military training and officer organization. Even colonies enhanced the training of troops to provide more effective fighting forces.

Another phenomenon that spread widely in the 19th century was the rise of nationalism and nationalist loyalties. Nationalism is the belief that a society has an identifiable national culture that is measurably different from other cultures. Cultural nationalists often assert that their nation's culture is better than others and may believe that the culture should be connected to the state. Nationalists typically argue that recognizable divisions exist among peoples based on different national traditions. Nationalism is a mostly modern phenomenon that contrasts with traditional types of loyalty to religion or locality.

Nationalism was born in Europe on the basis of two factors. Nationalism was an objection to Enlightenment thinking that argued that all peoples were fundamentally the same. Increased population movement and the rise of the new middle class created an audience for loyalty to an entity that was larger than the locality and would help uprooted peoples in the city find a sense of identity.

Nationalism received a significant boost from the French Revolution. By tearing down local institutions and reducing the power of the church, the French Revolution resulted in the idea that the government belonged to the people, who now owed it loyalty.

From Western and Central Europe, nationalism quickly spread in two additional directions, visible by the late-18th and early-19th centuries. It spread to the Americas, becoming more distinct after the American Revolution, and to Eastern Europe. In the Americas, nationalism was primarily used to form new states or to undergird new states and identities; in Eastern Europe, nationalism became a force to attack multinational empires.

Nationalism spread to the Middle East by the middle of the 19th century and to India by the 1880s; from the 1860s to 1900, we see nationalist elements in Japan, Russia, Turkey, and Africa. In other words, from the 1750s to 1914, nationalism was effectively created and gained some attention in virtually every part of the world.

What were the implications of nationalism? As we saw in Europe, nationalism provided new loyalties for people who were facing rapid economic and political change. Further, nationalism provided alternatives to traditional loyalties, particularly with regard to religion. Nationalism helped people entertain the possibility of a certain degree of change, while insisting that change had to be modified or controlled by attachment to tradition. Nationalists may also argue that in order to express national strength, certain kinds of changes are needed, such as more attention to industrial development or even changes in styles of dress to appear more businesslike. Hence, it could link directly to modernization.

Nationalism was an increasingly important rallying point for many peoples around the world against the West; national loyalties united people across traditional boundaries of class, caste, or even gender. ∎

Suggested Reading

Benedict Anderson, *Imagined Communities: Reflections on the Origin and Spread of Nationalism.*

Ronald Inglehart, *Modernization, Cultural Change, and Democracy: The Human Development Sequence.*

Robin W. Winks and Joan Neuberger, *Europe and the Making of Modernity, 1815–1914.*

Questions to Consider

1. Is the idea of limited modernization useful for world history in the 19th century? What are the main dangers of using the concept? Can modernization be distinguished from simple Westernization?

2. Why did nationalism often structure opposition to imperialism better than religion or sheer traditionalism?

Formation of Latin American Civilization
Lecture 27

From the colonial period, Latin America, which in many ways is the world's newest major civilization—although we'll need to talk about at least one other candidate—from the colonial experience, Latin America had developed a number of important features.

Crucial developments occurred in Latin America in the 19th century. The civilization had already been shaped by the interaction of Spanish/Portuguese, African, and Native American populations during the early modern period, in a context dominated by colonialism, the Colombian exchange, and Latin America's peripheral position in the world economy. Catholicism had spread widely, though with admixtures from traditional cultures.

The powers of colonial governments were limited, though reform efforts in the 18th century had some effect. The big news in the 19th century was the establishment of national independence, followed by some revealing political problems and a seesaw battle between liberalism and conservatism. Formal culture blossomed more fully, linked to Western models but with regional themes and flavors. New sources of immigration and a growing urban middle class enhanced ties with the West, as well. Dependent status in the world economy increased on the whole, despite vigorous efforts to the contrary; the growing hemispheric power of the United States figured into this mix.

We have sketched some general patterns of world history in this period: the force of the world economy as the West industrialized, the limited but measurable development of modernization, the force of Western military strength and imperialism, and the spread of national loyalties. In this lecture, we will look at these larger factors in the context of a particular civilization's experiences. One reason to focus on Latin America is a general concern in world history to pay appropriate attention to this region.

From the colonial period, Latin America had developed a number of important features. The Latin American economy depended, in many respects, on that of Western Europe through the intermediaries of Spain and Portugal, although by the 18th century, local manufacturing and other economic activities had emerged.

Latin America also faced significant issues concerning the formation of effective governments. Given the facts of colonial control by Spain and Portugal, economic interference from other sectors, and landlord rule in many parts of Latin America, developing effective central governments was a significant problem. Spain and Portugal had tried to address this issue during the 18th century in the so-called *Bourbon reforms*.

Latin American culture began to be forged in the colonial period, as well. Imports from Western Europe were predominant in the form of Catholicism and religious architectural and artistic forms. European priests and governors urged that Western standards be applied to families but in fact, partly because of colonial sexual exploitation of native women, large numbers of illegitimate children were present in Latin American families.

Among the events that shaped Latin American experience in the Long 19th Century were the wars of independence that stretched from 1810–1820. These independence movements reflected liberal and nationalist beliefs imported from Western Europe and the United States. The goals were independence from Spanish and Portuguese control and the formation of liberal political states featuring parliaments and constitutions; there was also some hope of curbing the Catholic Church's powers.

The social base of the independence movements was fairly shallow: most of the leadership was Creole, that is, people of European origin born in Latin America. Although a few regions saw reform, such as the abolition of slavery in Mexico, the social results of these movements were generally limited. The independence movements removed the Spanish but did not overturn the basic ruling forces in Latin American society that revolved around the church, the landlord class, and, increasingly, the military.

After independence was achieved, many Latin American nations exhibited a characteristic set of "new nations'" problems during the 1820s–1840s. One of the grievances of the independence leaders was that they had been excluded from participation in government, but by the same token, not many people were available who had experience in running a state. Another characteristic problem in the formation of new nations is at least a brief period of economic dislocation. In Latin America, this problem was exacerbated by the importation of British industrial goods after the withdrawal of Spanish tariff and military protection.

Disputes over political legitimacy were another predictable problem. Although most of the independence movements were hostile to monarchies, in certain regions, such as Mexico, monarchy seemed the most sensible system. Quarrels might also arise relating to the territorial integrity of the new states. Nationalist leaders in Latin America hoped to form large nations on the model of the United States. Most of these ambitious combinations fell apart, however, because the legitimacy of the territory was not recognized. In the process of settling boundaries, Latin America saw much political turmoil. External boundaries were often disputed in the formation of new nations.

The answer to the question "Is Latin American civilization Western?" is clearly mixed.

Certain outcomes are also characteristic of new nations' problems. The first of these is a tendency toward political instability, which we see clearly in 19th- and even 20th-century Latin America. We also note an ongoing tension between conservatives, bent on protecting the church and landlords, and liberals, interested in social reform, education, limitations on the church, and the creation of a parliamentary system.

Another common outcome is the phenomenon of *caudillismo*, that is, the selection of dictators whose rule promises to end instability. This aspect of Latin American history contrasts with the experience of the United States, also a new nation, but not one in which these problems occurred to the same degree. Different colonial experience had given more North Americans experience in government. The issue of slavery, however, would present a significant new problem to the United States.

The Long 19th Century was an important period for the development of Latin American culture. Latin America emerged from tentative cultural expressions to the potential for creating literary and artistic currents of its own. A number of Latin American novelists, for example, emerged in the 19th century and exploited characteristic Latin American themes of frontiers and ethnic diversity. At the same time, these novelists and other artists were still strongly influenced by literary and intellectual patterns developed in Western Europe and, to some extent, in the United States.

Western influences were apparent in some other respects that go beyond high culture. For example, in many Latin American countries, cities were expanded or created along European architectural lines. An urban middle class emerged in Latin America that often espoused European values, such as the new emphasis on public health measures or the efforts to impose Western standards on native populations. Increasing European immigration—to Argentina, Uruguay, Chile, and, to some extent, Brazil—furthered European influence. At the same time, however, people of Native American, Mestizo, or African origin continued to defend popular religious traditions and other cultural elements that reflected a somewhat different perspective.

Any discussion of Latin America in the Long 19th Century must note the growing peripheralization of the economy. By the middle of the 19th century, after the successful independence movements, many parts of Latin America saw the recovery of a certain degree of prosperity. From about 1870 onward, however, Latin America was marked by peripheralization.

An increasing number of peoples and territories were locked into the production of export goods, some of which were damaging to the environment. More segments of the Latin American economy now depended on cheap labor to produce goods for the export market. Exportation, in turn, supported imports of expensive processed goods or produced revenues only for the upper class.

A new component here was the difficulty faced by even reformers in pulling Latin America out of this peripheral relationship. Machinery for Latin American factories had to be imported from Western Europe or the United States and purchased with money borrowed from European or

American banks. International indebtedness made the dependent status of the Latin American economy harder to remedy. To pay for the importation of equipment, the obvious recourse was to increase production of exports.

To expand coffee production, it was necessary to press farther into the interior, which meant that railroads were needed to bring the product to market. To build railways, however, stock had to be purchased from industrial societies. This effort to increase production actually drove down prices, making it impossible for Latin America to pull out of economic dependency.

The developments in Latin America illustrate the variety of historical experiences that a major society could have in the Long 19th Century. Along with the economic dependency we have just discussed could come significant political innovation: not only the achievement of independence but the emergence of new political movements and the capacity to foster social and cultural reforms.

Bridge in the sublime Infurnillo gorge, Peru. Latin America had to press farther into the interior to support an expanding production of exports.

Latin Americans themselves sometimes debate the experiences of the Long 19th Century and earlier colonial precedence by questioning whether Latin America was a Western civilization. On the affirmative side are aspects of the civilization's high culture, in which we see a Latin American contribution to the common Western intellectual enterprise. On the side of complexity is the extent to which Latin American developments tended to be stronger in the humanities than science. In popular culture, Latin America was home to a number of vigorous popular religious movements that differed considerably from their European counterparts.

Western liberal and nationalist ideals appeared in Latin American politics, but the instability in this arena was somewhat greater in Latin America than in Europe. When we look at economic patterns, the picture does not look particularly Western at all. The question of whether Latin American civilization was Western can help organize our comparisons, but it entails complexities that reflect both earlier traditions and new aspects of the Latin American experience during the Long 19th Century. ■

Suggested Reading

Sylvia Chant and Nikki Craske, *Gender in Latin America*.

Carlos Forment, *Democracy in Latin America, 1760–1900,* vol. 1: *Civic Selfhood and Public Life in Mexico and Peru*.

Mark Thurner and Andres Guerrero, eds., *After Spanish Rule: Postcolonial Predicaments of the Americas*.

Questions to Consider

1. Did the United States largely avoid the new nations' problems visible in Latin America? If so, why? What factors differentiated Latin America from the U.S. experience of independence?

2. By the end of the Long 19th Century, was Latin America part of Western civilization, or is it analytically preferable to see it as a separate civilization—the newest, to date, in world history?

China and Japan—19th-Century Pressures
Lecture 28

Our discussion today focuses on comparing Japanese and Chinese developments in the Long 19th Century, particularly from the 1840s–1850s onward. The comparison is interesting in several respects.

China and Japan shared many characteristics, largely because of Japan's long period of imitation. Yet their reactions to new Western pressure and the changing dynamics of the world economy were strikingly different, establishing two separate East Asian models whose impact is still felt today. Comparison here reveals a history important to East Asia but also suggests some of the wider forces operating in the Long 19th Century: some societies sought to emulate Japan while others responded in terms more similar to those of China.

Japan, once forced to open more fully to the wider world, quickly embarked on major changes, while also demonstrating the possibility of modernizing without fully Westernizing. China long resisted pressures to reform, yielding only incompletely after 1900 when, to many observers, it already seemed too late. The causes and the results of this East Asian differentiation are significant to the course of world history over the past two centuries.

A number of societies can be brought together to examine how 19th-century factors were shaped by particular experiences. Japan and Russia constitute an interesting comparison. Both of these fundamentally non-Western societies launched significant industrial revolutions by the 1890s, although the processes of doing so differed.

The Japanese-Chinese comparison is fruitful for a number of reasons. There is a marked contrast between a society that introduced successful reforms (Japan) and a society that was unusually laggard (China). Nonetheless, these two societies shared many features. The close interaction of Japan and China raises the question of why one experience would differ so much from the other. This comparison reveals significant implications for the 20th and even 21st centuries.

Both Japan and China were essentially forced to address the fact of new Western power by developments in the middle of the 19th century. The first Opium War, beginning in 1839, revealed the capability of Western military forces to unseat Chinese policy intentions and traditions. The Chinese also realized that the West was so eager to gain access to Chinese wealth and markets that it would push virtually any product that would accomplish this end.

Japan's introduction to Western power took place a little later. The arrival of Western fleets from 1853 onward was a statement that if Japan did not open its markets, the Western powers would come in force. Military clashes occurred between Western forces and those of Japan. The West imposed constraints on Japanese activity that would ease only in the early-20th century. Thus, forced entry and unwelcome intrusion are factors in both cases.

China, with its great political tradition, might have reacted more successfully to this intrusion than Japan. The Chinese also had technological superiority and greater natural resources than Japan. As both societies were forced into change, Japan might have been expected to have more difficulty.

Japan did, of course, have some assets. In the 18th century, it had begun to open itself to foreign influence. It moved clearly toward dissemination of education.

Beginning in 1868, Japan launched a series of reforms in what is called the *Meiji era* (*Meiji* meaning "enlightened"). The Meiji era included reforms in an impressive variety of categories, beginning with politics. In 1868, the feudal system was abolished, and the Japanese gradually developed a system of parliamentary monarchy with a constitution based on limited suffrage. Japan also saw the emergence of a new elite that would come to dominate government.

Early in the process, Japan began to create a European-style military structure with a modern navy and upgraded technology. Japanese infrastructure was modernized; railroad networks were established that, along with shipping, unified the Japanese islands. Meanwhile, Japanese enthusiasm for new public health measures permitted rapid expansion of the population. In 1872, the Japanese mandated a mass education system for both boys and girls. Educational reform included modifications of the Confucian intellectual approach, which tended to emphasize tradition over creative thinking and scientific innovation. Schooling was provided in modern languages, including English and German. The Japanese enthusiasm for change extended to consumer items, such as toothpaste. By 1900, department stores were established in Tokyo.

These reforms did not represent a complete cave-in to Westernization. In the 1880s, Japan pulled back from creating a Western educational system, introducing textbooks that focused on Japanese traditions. But these reforms did include a massive effort at industrialization. By the 1890s, Japan was beginning to establish a significant factory system with a strong emphasis on export production. Japanese industrialization was stimulated by high taxes on the peasantry, which helped free up funds for investment, and by poor working conditions. The capacity to seize much of the silk export market from the Chinese provided vital opportunities for foreign earnings and capital formation in Japan that would fuel a more general industrial development. By the second decade of the 20th century, Japan would move into heavy industrialization, a process that would ultimately yield a share of world industrial leadership to the Japanese by the second half of the 20th century.

In China, where there was no clear decision to embark on reform, the pattern was vastly different. The first railway line built in China by a private company was torn up by the government in a show of resistance to progress and imitation. The Chinese were modestly interested in Western military innovations, but they did not organize the kinds of military and political changes that would allow them to catch up to Western standards. China's responses to modernization were further complicated by internal unrest and civil war in the middle of the 19th century.

China's reactions were also hampered by the tendency of the Western powers and Russia to seize chunks of Chinese territory, where they then developed industry. These intrusions reduced Chinese economic capacity and increased hostility to foreigners. The Boxer Rebellion would be an understandable manifestation of this anti-foreign hostility.

Only in the 1890s did the Chinese begin to come to terms with the new situation. Chinese university students began to go to Japan and the United States; Christian missionary activity established new educational institutions in China; and traditional practices, such as foot-binding, declined. Unfortunately, this reaction was late and incomplete.

Why does the experience of China contrast so markedly with that of Japan? Western encroachments on China were much more unsettling than those on Japan, partly because the West had an older, historical thirst for Chinese access. The Japanese produced some goods the West wanted, but there was less pent-up demand for interference.

Western intervention also caught Japan and China in different phases of the political cycle. The Chinese were in one of their periodic political doldrums, which meant that Western intrusion was less effectively opposed. The Tokugawa shogunate had some problems of social unrest and difficulty collecting sufficient tax revenues, but the Japanese state encountered the West at a point of greater strength. Although Japan and China both operated within a Confucian tradition, Japanese Confucianism was somewhat less traditionalist, less bent on absolute resistance to foreign influence, and more interested in spreading the benefits of education than the system in China.

Japanese feudalism, which had been absent for some time from the Chinese tradition, may also have created an advantage for Japan. The extent to which feudal classes remained in Japan gave that nation a quicker appreciation of the military aspects of the Western challenge than occurred in China, where the military had less voice. Japanese feudalism may also have created group loyalties that could be used for industrialization and political action.

Japan had a history of successful imitation, and China did not. From their earlier interactions with China, the Japanese knew that it was possible to imitate without losing cultural identity or surrendering to foreigners. China's major experience of imitation, the importation of Buddhism, had ended badly, as had its experience with the Mongols.

The Japanese borrowed from the West while controlling Western influences much more effectively than any other non-Western society in the Long 19th Century. The Japanese regulated Western ownership during industrialization and modified Western influence by maintaining traditions of group loyalty and emperor worship.

A somewhat less concrete but also very real result of the different paths of Japan and China in the Long 19th Century involves social stability.

By the end of the Long 19th Century, the differences between Japan and China had significant consequences. In the 1890s, Japan and China went to war, and the Japanese, with their modern military and industrial strength, won fairly handily. One result of the conflict was a pattern of ongoing Japanese influence in Korea.

Japan would soon also confront Russia in the Russo-Japanese War of 1904–1905. Again the Japanese won. Russia, although industrializing, remained a more cumbersome society and had more trouble bringing military force to bear in the Pacific than did the Japanese. Power balances shifted as the Japanese began to make their own claim to global power. Comparative differences between Japan and China were translated into ongoing military hostilities, extending into renewed Japanese attacks on China in the 1930s and into World War II and beyond.

A somewhat less concrete result of the different paths of Japan and China in the Long 19th Century involves social stability. Japan's reform experience, including its industrialization, created massive social tension. In China, many leaders believed that the only way to mount a successful response to Western intrusion was through outright revolution.

The Japanese experience at the end of the Long 19th Century was unique. Japan experienced modernization without full Westernization and would become an important addition to the roster of industrial and military powers of the modern world. The Chinese sluggishness in responding to outside challenge was greater than that of many other societies but, in many ways, more typical. Many societies had difficulty addressing the implications of Western power for effective political and economic operation at home. The Chinese deficit here, however, was not permanent. When we introduce the final period in world history in the next lecture, we will see not only the significance of Japan's ongoing role but the growing muscle of China in world affairs, as well. ■

Suggested Reading

Michael Gasster, *China's Struggle to Modernize*.

John Sagers, *Origins of Japanese Wealth and Power: Reconciling Confucianism and Capitalism, 1830–1885*.

Rudra Sil, Managing "Modernity": Work, Community, and Authority in Late-Industrializing Japan and Russia.

Questions to Consider

1. What are the main ways in which Japan proved to be a case of successful modernizing without fully Westernizing?

2. What was the relationship between China's "failure to modernize" and the emergence of a revolutionary process in 1910?

The 20ᵗʰ–21ˢᵗ Centuries as a New Period
Lecture 29

> Indeed, the period is best known as the contemporary period because, although it began in the 20ᵗʰ century, in most respects, it seems to be continuing into the 21ˢᵗ—for how long, we obviously don't know.

The 20ᵗʰ century meets the two basic definitions of a new period: themes dominant in the previous period are no longer dominant, and major new themes surface. The 20ᵗʰ century divides into three sub-periods: the decades dominated by world wars and depression; the postwar years, highlighted by decolonization and the Cold War; and the now almost two post–Cold War decades. Beginning with World War I, the military and political dominance of the West began to erode—two of the themes that had most clearly shaped the Long 19ᵗʰ Century.

The world wars greatly weakened the West, accelerating international demands for independence. Even the West's economic dominance, though more clearly sustained, began to be qualified by new competitors, particularly from the Pacific Rim. As old themes faded, new ones surfaced. Politically, almost every regime operating in 1900 was replaced at least once; the decline of monarchy and empire was striking. Simultaneously, the landholding aristocracy was displaced as the preeminent social class.

The Hubble Space Telescope.

New types of warfare and space travel might also be advanced as defining themes, though to date, some caution might be warranted here. The two leading new themes, to which every major society had to react, were unprecedented global population growth and the new technological and organizational capacity for global contacts. Population explosion and its attendant migration had obvious political and environmental effects, helping to unseat older regimes. A steady stream of connective technologies supported the emergence of new organizational forms, such as the multinational corporation. These themes supplanted the preeminence of the West in shaping the new world history era.

As we look at developments over the past century, we must be careful to maintain contact with earlier patterns, with characteristics of the individual major civilizations, and with earlier processes in world history. In studying change in the contemporary period, we risk ignoring the fact that this period does not stand in isolation to the past. Although the contemporary period is new, some features, such as the cultural, political, economic, and military power of the West, are carryovers from the Long 19th Century and even earlier. The world economy also persisted in some ways, and modernization blossomed further in this period.

Two key issues in dealing with the contemporary period involve the currency and complexity of developments over the past century and the fact that we do not know the end of the story. We can point to changes from patterns in the Long 19th Century, but we cannot always say that new patterns are well established, and we cannot make final determinations about new directions.

The 20th and early-21st centuries are usually divided into three phases. The years 1914–1945 were dominated by two world wars, the Depression, disarray in Western society, stirrings in other societies, and the force of new revolutions, particularly in the Soviet Union. The years 1945–1990 were marked by the Cold War, which provides an alternative to the main frame of reference that applied to the world war and interwar period. With the collapse of the Soviet Union and the end of the Cold War, we enter the third phase of the contemporary era, marked, perhaps, by the emergence of the United States as "the world's only superpower," along with some questions about how long that role would last.

The two world wars posed new questions about the Western role in the world, particularly the West European role. We see a decline of Western Europe in world affairs, particularly after World War II; this decline opened a transitional framework in which the Soviet Union and the United States disputed world dominance. That transitional system failed, and the Cold War became a first statement about how to address the shifting world power balance. In the third phase of the contemporary era, we are involved in more open-ended questions about what the new power structure will be.

It is important to remember that the contemporary period is still a recent one in world history; some of the details have yet to be worked out, and some of the new themes have yet to be fully established.

What are the new themes in the contemporary period? The dominant social class in most societies in 1900 or 1914 was still the landed aristocracy. By the early-21st century, the aristocracy is almost gone, replaced by a new kind of professional middle class. This social class thinks of the world more in industrial than in agricultural terms, more in urban terms than in rural, and more in managerial structures than in terms of private land ownership.

In 1900 or 1910, the world's major political regimes were predominantly monarchies or empires, but these systems are largely gone in the early-21st century. The alternatives include democracies, along with authoritarian regimes and communist systems. Gender relationships also seem to enter a new phase in the contemporary era. Older systems of patriarchy were modified by efforts to give women the vote, improve their educational levels, and provide them with some legal rights.

The gender system that would replace the patriarchal system, however, has not been clearly defined. The new system is not completely egalitarian and does not fully address women's economic role or the issue of male violence against women. The contemporary period is partly defined by shifts in gender relations, but the themes here have not been fully established.

The contemporary period offers a new set of challenges to older cultural beliefs; these challenges come from communism, a greater mass appeal of nationalism, consumerism, and science. In important ways these cultural options do not entirely agree with one another. By the early-21st century, these options had not fully succeeded in displacing the old. The cultural map of the contemporary period is complicated; we cannot say for sure that the older patterns have been vanquished.

In defining the contemporary period, we must look at the shift away from dominant patterns of the Long 19th Century and, to some extent, aspects of the early modern period. We begin by looking at the relative decline of the West, for which we see evidence beginning in World War I. Both world wars, apart from their global dimensions, can be seen as a giant internal civil war within the West. In this conflict, the West's inability to maintain its power position in the world accelerated as a result of the economic, political, and population damage Western societies inflicted on one another. The measurements of relative decline important here are found in the military and in the West's capacity to control most other parts of the world.

> **Some centuries hence people may look back at the contemporary period of world history and say, "Ah, the fundamental innovation in this period was the beginning of humankind's conquest of outer space."**

In the early-21st century, the West still possessed the greatest military power in the world as a whole. But the capacity of the West to move almost at will militarily had been curtailed by the second half of the 20th century. One reason for this was that Western countries became less willing to invest heavily in maintaining cutting-edge military technologies. Several other parts of the world began to emphasize military tactics that could stalemate the West's advantage in conventional armament—such as guerilla warfare in Vietnam or the resistance in urban settings seen in Algeria and Iraq. As individual countries gained independence and a measure of economic success, they invested in military force. The West could still defeat such countries, but doing so took much more planning and economic commitment than previously.

We also see decline in the West's capacity to control most of the rest of the world directly through colonies and colonial administrations. One key development in the contemporary period, starting between the wars and accelerating after World War II, was decolonization. Western political and economic influence could survive decolonization in some cases, but the world as a whole saw a much reduced capacity of any single civilization or society to dominate global politics. Some people argue that the relative decline of the West will ultimately yield predominance to another civilization but there is no inherent reason that a pattern of successive dominance must repeat itself.

Several other themes began to gain ascendancy in the contemporary period. In future centuries, people may see the fundamental innovation of the contemporary period as the beginning of humankind's conquest of outer space. In the early-21st century, however, space exploration has not yet had a deep impact on human life or the patterns of global societies.

Another candidate for the contemporary period's fundamental innovation is the altered nature of war and military technology in the 21st century. The two world wars introduced the concept of *total war*—the mobilization of all the major resources of the key combatants, not just armies and navies but the economy and civilians, as well. World War II gave birth to the capability to end human existence with nuclear weapons. Among the new themes of the contemporary era were the tightened organizational capacity in war, societies' insistence on total surrender as a result of their investment, and the threat of devastating and fearsome new technology.

Another theme of the contemporary period is massive global population increase. This population growth carries over into other features that begin to reshape the world. World population explosion encourages new patterns of immigration, bringing together people from different cultural backgrounds and leading to new challenges in many societies. Population explosion also places unprecedented stress on global environments.

The final defining theme involves the steady acceleration of communication and transportation technologies. Important developments here include radio, satellite communications, the Internet, and air travel. These technologies offer unprecedented opportunities and, in some ways, pose unprecedented threats and challenges to the identities of individual societies. The accelerated movement of ideas, goods, and peoples, sometimes referred to as *globalization*, is an indisputable mark of the new period of world history.

In the next lecture, we will turn to changes in the world economy, where we will find echoes of the themes we have discussed here and, again, significant change but no certainty about the outcomes. ∎

Suggested Reading

Eric Hobsbawm, *The Age of Extremes: A History of the World, 1914–1991*.

Sally Marks, *The Ebbing of European Ascendancy: An International History of the World, 1914–1945*.

Peter N. Stearns, *Consumerism in World History: The Global Transformation of Desire*.

Theodore von Laue, *The World Revolution of Westernization: The Twentieth Century in Global Perspective*.

Questions to Consider

1. Given the West's ongoing cultural, political, and economic influence and the role of the United States as an essentially Western power, is the relative decline of the West a valid historical theme for the contemporary period of world history?

2. How do the advent of nuclear weaponry and the changing nature of war fit into a definition of the new period in world history?

The World Economy—Change and Continuity
Lecture 30

We're talking in this session about the world economy in the contemporary period of world history, 20th–early 21st centuries. This is a fascinating opportunity to note continuity in world history between the Long 19th Century, or even early modern/Long 19th Century and contemporary, but ultimately, also to talk about change.

One of the frameworks for world history from the early modern period onward has been the unequal relationships in world trade. The dominance of the industrial West in the Long 19th Century was a crucial factor for literally every society in the world. In the contemporary period, elements of the now-traditional world economy persisted. The basic definition of the core economies survived, though now with primary emphasis on high-tech, service, and entertainment products.

Peripheral or dependent economies dotted the landscape; the increasing peripheralization of much of Africa was a key development during the 20th century. The addition of Japan and the Pacific Rim to the list of core economies was another crucial development. Another change was intriguing though shorter-lived: at various points in the mid-20th century, a variety of societies sought to escape the world economy, setting up separate economic zones. This was an interesting comment on the downside of the world economy previously, but also on some increase in the latitude available to escape Western domination.

The most important general shift, marking a new stage in the evolution of the world economy, was the capacity of many societies to gain some relief from the worst inferiorities of the world economy and to introduce new sources of profit. This process began in the 1920s but reached fuller fruition toward the end of the century. From Brazil to China, a number of countries once included in an undifferentiated Third World status managed, without achieving full equality with the core, to become major international players. Forecasts suggested that this trend would continue into the global future.

The term *Third World*, in some ways, seems to enshrine continuity. Over time, this term came to refer to parts of the world that were not industrialized and were vastly poorer than the First World. The world economy concept itself, as enunciated by Wallerstein, was meant to enshrine persistence. Wallerstein's point was that the origins of the fatal economic gaps that persisted in the contemporary world could be found in the early modern period and the 19th century.

Core characteristics can still be identified in the 21st century in much of Western Europe and the United States. These societies still export expensive goods and import cheaper goods, using trading companies based in the core. They rely on wage labor and have, for the most part, stable governments. Their goods, however, have changed; they now export professional services and many entertainment staples.

A few societies did not display core characteristics in terms of export-import but managed to maintain fairly high standards of living. These societies fit a semi-core definition. Canada, for example, was a leading raw materials and food supplier to the United States. Australia, by the later-20th century, was the leading raw materials supplier to Japan.

Peripheries were still characterized by relatively weak governments and continued to export cheap goods, such as lower-level manufactured products. Some of the locations of the periphery shifted. Peripheral societies still existed in Latin America and Central America, where cheap factory products and drugs were exported. The key periphery during the contemporary period, however, could be found in sub-Saharan Africa, where food supplies, raw materials, and mining supplies were the predominant exports. Although Africa had been colonized by the end of the Long 19th Century, it was only in the 20th century that its economy was converted more fully to peripheral status by the operations of colonial powers.

The most striking shift in the contemporary period was the entry into the core of Japan, followed by other parts of the Pacific Rim, including South Korea and Taiwan. This development modified the association of the core with the West; thus, when we think about the relative decline of the West, we must consider the fact that Western Europe's monopoly over core status was qualified by the addition of parts of East Asia. A second cultural zone was now capable of advanced industrialization and participation in the core. Japan, South Korea, and Taiwan imitated Western countries in many respects, but they maintained a Confucian emphasis on group loyalty, group values, collective decision-making, and close relationships between the state and the private sector.

Earlier patterns seem to be persistent in the contemporary period. Some societies still reap disproportionate benefits from world trade, while some labor under disadvantages. The only things that seem to have changed are the geography, some of the entrants in both camps, and the specific goods exchanged.

This emphasis on persistence, however, misses the clear beginnings of efforts to move away from the world economic framework in several ways. Beginning early in the 20th century, a number of societies saw that the world economy was not working to their benefit; they needed to establish their own market frameworks that would release them from dependence on global economic relationships. The first country that came to this realization was Russia, where the doctrine of socialism under Stalin proclaimed that the Soviet Union could industrialize without significant contact with the rest of the world. Soviet economic growth, however, came at the cost of low wages, social frustration, and environmental damage.

In the 1960s, China attempted a similar isolation. After the Communist Revolution was completed in 1949, China's industrialization was meant to proceed in conjunction with the Soviet Union's. Later, however, China moved toward an even more isolationist policy. As World War II neared, Japanese attempts to establish relationships with a colonial sphere in East and Southeast Asia represented another effort at partial economic isolation. Japan envisioned what it called the *co-prosperity sphere*, in which a set of countries would trade with Japan in unequal relationships.

Nazi Germany, to some extent, also sought to separate itself from the world economy. The goal was for Germany to set up a colonial relationship with the agricultural regions of Eastern Europe and, again, launch a mini-world economy in which German industrial might was supported by cheap exports from the Slavic hinterland. This interlude is echoed even in the 21st century by small cases of economic isolation, most notably in North Korea.

By the later-20th century, most of the societies that had tried the go-it-alone policy had concluded that it was a mistake and, one by one, rejoined the world economy.

The more durable efforts to adjust to the world economy in ways that complicate the core-periphery relationships fall into several categories. Peripheral societies are characterized by low-wage economies, a small capitalist class, and intense pressure for more sophisticated exports. Elements of peripheralization, in the sense of low-wage export sectors, still exist in the economies we will discuss.

The first method used to help countries climb out of peripheralization was the policy of *import substitution*, initiated in the 1920s. Under this policy, the government, working with private entrepreneurs, sets up production of some essential but less sophisticated industrial products, such as textiles, automobiles, and basic appliances; these products, then, no longer have to be imported from the core. This move does not totally break the core-periphery relationship, but it reduces the importation of expensive items; import substitution is also usually accompanied by protective tariffs.

Many economists question the long-term utility of these measures, but in the short run they can help moderate dependency. Latin American countries, suffering from the Great Depression, moved toward import substitution in the mid- to late 1930s; India would adopt measures of import substitution after it achieved independence in 1947. The goods produced for import substitution were not necessarily of as high quality as those produced by the core, but these products satisfied part of local demand and reduced economic pressure.

Another method used to escape peripheralization was to seize on one particular good that was either valuable or could be produced in newly efficient ways and translated into exports; the most obvious case in point here is Middle Eastern oil, initially a peripheral product. When Western companies controlled the supply, oil was essentially a cheap product. Once independence was achieved by major Middle Eastern and North African nations after World War II, however, political measures could be used to seize control of the oil and make it a very profitable export. This is what happened in the Gulf states in the decades since the 1950s. Other products could be used, as well; Chile, for example, by the 1970s and 1980s, was breaking out of the peripheral trap by emphasizing vegetable and fruit production for U.S. markets.

The third method to break out of peripheralization was to develop a few sectors in which an economy could begin to compete with the core—by exporting processed goods on a worldwide basis. Brazil, for example, negotiated with the United States during World War II for the provision of a modern steel industry in return for American use of Brazilian observation posts. The Brazilians also became aware of the military implications of the computer industry fairly early, and the government began to sponsor investments in computers. The Brazilian economy continues to have pockets of poverty and many peripheral industries and agricultural sectors, but it has moved out of an easily definable category.

Increasingly, by the 21st century, the key issues were actually not so much among regions but within them.

By the 1990s and the early years of the 21st century, the big stories in export sectors were, of course, China and India. China became, almost literally, the workshop of the world. Wages were low and workers were exploited, but the capacity to produce textiles, electronics, gifts, and other basic goods makes it impossible now to define China as a peripheral economy. India's transformation involved less emphasis on global manufacturing and more on the development of service industries. A host of societies, by using one or more of these innovative methods, have thus complicated their categorization in the world economy.

The contemporary period continues elements inherited from the Long 19th Century, but it puts its own stamp on these patterns. By the later-20th and early-21st centuries, we see what some economists are calling the industrialization of the world. In the late-20th century, about 20 percent of the world's population was actively involved in industrializing economies; this number has jumped to 60 percent in the early-21st century. The inequality of economic relationships among different parts of the world is not gone, but by the 21st century the key issues were not so much among regions as within them, generated by the process of partial industrialization and import substitution. ■

Suggested Reading

Ben Schneider, *Business Politics and the State in Twentieth-Century Latin America.*

Vera Simone and Anne Thompson Feraru, *The Asian Pacific: Political and Economic Development in a Global Context.*

Questions to Consider

1. Why did some societies choose to insulate themselves from the world economy? Why was it more possible to do this in the 20th century than in the late-19th century?

2. What factors should be considered in trying to decide whether, during the past century, international economic inequality has increased or decreased?

An Age of Revolutions

Lecture 31

Revolutions began in the second decade of the century and continued at least until the 1980s. Our discussion today focuses on the revolutions themselves in terms of their basic dynamics and ... the ways in which they actually helped launch these changes, particularly in the societies directly affected but, to some degree, more widely.

The 20th century saw an unprecedented number of political and social revolutions. These were a key part of the larger process of political and social change. Major revolutions included the Russian, Chinese, Mexican, and Iranian revolutions, but there were also revolutions during the 1950s and 1970s in Bolivia, Egypt, Vietnam, Cuba, Nicaragua, and elsewhere. Industrialized and newly decolonized nations were largely exempt, but otherwise, the process, though hardly universal, was widespread.

Revolutions resulted from peasant discontent, inept political repression, new ideologies, and resentment of Western influence or control. Liberal strands were less prominent than in the Atlantic revolutions around the turn of the 19th century. Revolutions generated authoritarian regimes for a considerable time, efforts at cultural change, curtailment of the traditional upper class, and some limitations on Western influence, though the range of consequences varied considerably.

Revolutions also pushed more established regimes, particularly the United States, toward greater conservatism. Revolutions did not define the whole of 20th-century world history, but they contributed to major changes even outside the societies directly affected. At the end of the 20th century, a somewhat more peaceful spread of democracy raised questions about the future need for revolutionary outbreaks.

A revolution is a violent attempt to change the political system, introduce new social layers into the system, and effect social change. A revolution differs from a coup d'état, which can be significant in an individual society but does not bring about fundamental changes. In the 20th century, we must differentiate between revolutions and wars of independence. Significant independence struggles took place in the 20th century, but they were not revolutions in the sense of using violence to undertake a thorough political and social cleansing. The 20th-century revolutions involved many parts of the world, including parts of Eastern Europe, Asia, Latin America, and the Middle East. This geographical spread represents the extent to which activities that previously were regional now became global.

The 20th century saw four major revolutions. The first revolution was the Mexican revolution in 1910–1920, reflecting a variety of grievances and involving a variety of groups. Middle-class liberals involved in the Mexican revolution sought political and constitutional reforms; peasant revolutionaries, such as Pancho Villa, were interested in land reforms. The goals of the Mexican revolution were varied,

Vladimir Lenin, founder of the Russian Communist Party.

and it took a decade of recurrent revolutionary activity for a settlement to be reached. The revolution ultimately resulted in limited land reforms, the installation of a one-party political system that provided political coherence, and genuine but noncompetitive elections. The Mexican revolution was unusual in having limited direct influence elsewhere.

The second revolution was the Chinese Revolution. Beginning in 1911, a group of middle-class revolutionary students and intellectuals overthrew the imperial system. Initial efforts to establish a Western-style parliamentary democracy were hampered by the power claims of regional warlords and landlords, by the invasion of the Japanese, and by divisions among Chinese revolutionaries. The new communist movement that was born in the early 1920s would ultimately prevail in China in 1949.

The third great revolution was the Soviet revolution in 1917. The Communist Revolution was inspired by Russia's hardships in World War I, longstanding peasant and worker grievances, and widespread concern about the police and authoritarian measures of the tsarist regime. In 1917, the Bolsheviks took over and launched a period of significant political, social, and cultural upheaval.

The fourth revolution, the Iranian revolution of 1979, was hailed at the time as possibly the first great Third World revolution. It was not dependent on Western ideas of any sort but was an Islamic revolution against undue Western influence and against an authoritarian and corrupt political regime. It urged a return to more fundamental Islamic political principles. It was meant to inspire a wave of similar revolutions in other societies.

In addition to these major revolutions, the 20th century, particularly after World War II, was peppered by other revolutionary surges in smaller areas. The 1950s, for example, saw revolution in Egypt, Bolivia, and Cuba. The 1970s saw revolution in Nicaragua. Vietnam constituted a revolution as well as a war for independence.

Major upheavals take some time to work out in terms of attainment of revolutionary goals and adjustment of the society. This process may still be occurring in some of the 20th-century cases. Revolutions never change everything; they always preserve significant segments of the "old regime"; the Russian Revolution, for example, replicated some of the tsarist interests.

The core components of 20th-century revolutions add up to four basic points. The first component is a weak regime; revolutions do not occur against vigorous regimes, even if they are corrupt and unjust in other respects.

Second, every revolution needs at least one large group with elements who believe that violence is justified to achieve legitimate social ends; in 20th-century revolutions, the most consistent provider of this muscle was the peasantry plus, in some cases, the working class in cities.

A third component of 20th-century revolution involves what might be called an *ideological buildup*; before the revolution, crucial ideologies are disseminated that help inspire revolutionary leaders. In Mexico, early China, and very early Russia, some revolutionaries were inspired by liberal and democratic principles. In Iran, the dominant ideology was a restatement of what some leaders believed to be the fundamentals of Islam. The dominant revolutionary ideology of the 20th century—operative in Russia, China, Vietnam, Cuba, and elsewhere—was Marxism, which called for an overthrow of the existing system by the working class. The fourth component in the 20th-century revolutions was some degree of concern about undue Western ownership and influence; we see this concern in Iran, Mexico, and Russia.

What did the 20th-century revolutions accomplish? 20th-century revolutions, although they might have intended otherwise, uniformly produced authoritarian regimes. Major revolutions inevitably result in internal backlash: aristocrats, conservatives, and sometimes religious leaders begin to organize military movements against the revolution, and this action in turn induces the revolutionaries to impose authority. In many revolutions, significant foreign resistance is evident, which again inspires revolutionary leaders to lean toward authoritarian control to defend the revolution against its enemies. These impulses toward authoritarianism occurred quicker and more fully in the 20th-century cases than had been true in the Atlantic revolutionary period.

A key question, which is important to evoke but, frankly, unanswerable, is whether the age of 20th-century revolution is now over with the 20th century itself.

Another major consequence of the 20th-century revolutions was social change. The communist revolutions in Russia and China, for example, eliminated the landlord class, sometimes with brutality and sometimes with "reeducation" or political discipline.

Revolutions in the 20th century uniformly attempted cultural reconditioning to reorient cultural signals inherited from the past. One of the triumphs of the Mexican revolution, for example, was the emergence of a new popular culture embellished by artistic and architectural efforts to pay homage to the

Indian heritage of Mexico and to the importance of workers and peasants. The communist revolutions would spend much time emphasizing cultural reeducation and new artistic principles under the banner of socialist realism.

Finally, all the revolutions, though to different degrees, reduced Western influence, at least for a time, and offered opportunities for political power to new groups of people. Those from worker or peasant backgrounds did not necessarily run the show, but there was significant political mobility and, with this, a surge of new blood, new interest, and new abilities to connect the revolutionary regime with ordinary people.

Revolutions occurred in some places, not all. Revolutions have not yet occurred, for the most part, in countries that experienced an independence struggle during the 20th century or in successfully industrialized societies. Nevertheless, revolutions have influence beyond their borders. Marxist movements, for example, compel significant attention even in societies where revolutions have not broken out, as we see in India and Africa. Revolutions help engender other types of protest movements and may also push regimes, as a means of avoiding revolution, into political and social change that might not otherwise be undertaken.

Twentieth-century revolutions helped create a new conservative block among world powers, ultimately headed by the United States. The Unites States undoubtedly entered the 20th century with a sense of its own revolutionary heritage and a certain sympathy for revolutionary strivings. From the Mexican and the Russian revolutions onward, however, Americans became concerned about the impact of revolution on American property rights and values and the potential for the importation of revolutionary movements into the United States.

Is the age of 20th-century revolution now over? Despite significant movements, such as the anti-apartheid struggle or the collapse of communism, we have seen no major revolutionary outbreaks for at least 20 years. The influence of Marxism as an inspirational ideology has diminished and will probably not be revived. As the world becomes more urban, the peasantry has almost disappeared. These changes might suggest that the current era of revolution is over, although revolution may well recur at some later stage. In examining contemporary world history, what's important to remember is that, even if the age of revolution has passed, revolutions provided a significant spur to change in a number of countries and a number of regions beyond the revolutions themselves. ∎

Suggested Reading

Theda Skocpol, *States and Social Revolutions: A Comparative Analysis of France, Russia and China.*

Jonathan Spence, *The Gate of Heavenly Peace: The Chinese and Their Revolution, 1895–1980.*

Rex Wade, *The Russian Revolution, 1917.*

Questions to Consider

1. Given the causes of 20th-century revolution and recent social and political changes around the world, is it reasonable to assume that the wave of contemporary revolutions has ended?

2. Why do revolutions characteristically generate authoritarian regimes, and why was this trend stronger in the 20th century than before?

The United States in World History

Lecture 32

The subject today is placing the United States in world history, and the main way to do this is to talk about certain types of issues that don't always have clear resolution but that need to be discussed in order to figure out how to make this connection.

At various points, pundits hailed the 20th century as the "American century," and although this is a bit of an exaggeration, it is clear that the U.S. role in the world increased fairly steadily. This constitutes a major feature in the contemporary period of world history to date. The development also raises some intriguing analytical questions about how to "insert" the United States given that American history is usually taught separately from world history and many world historians feel they already have enough to do without adding another country.

This lecture explores the issues involved, with principal focus on the U.S. world role as it evolved in contemporary world history. The first issue involves chronology: when does inclusion of the United States become inescapable in a world history course? The second issue involves status as a civilization: should the United States be treated as a civilization all its own (or maybe as a major part of a *settler society* category that would include Canada and Australia), or is it part of Western civilization? Americans themselves oscillate on this issue.

Finally, as the United States becomes more important in world affairs, what if any distinctive contributions does it make compared to its West European progenitors? Is the world really different for having the United States rather than Western Europe as a leading power? This lecture raises issues rather than offering definitive solutions; an understanding of the terms of debate is particularly important here.

Over the past 10–15 years, world historians have realized that the United States is too important a player in world historical activities to leave out of the picture. In this lecture, we will see how we can fit the United States in with other societies, particularly in the contemporary period.

Another issue we must confront is that most U.S. history is taught with an exceptionalist approach. In this approach, the experience of being in America is said to have created a separate set of trajectories and an exception to European patterns, despite significant earlier European influences in America. This exceptionalism is a legitimate stance if it is approached analytically; too often, however, it is merely asserted.

The first issue we'll examine is chronological: at what point in time does the involvement of the United States on the world stage become so significant that the country must be included in the study of world history? In the colonial period, the United States was a slave recipient, but slave imports to what became the United States constituted less than $1/10^{th}$ of the total traffic across the Atlantic. The colonies contributed to the world economy, especially the South, and the United States received a certain amount of immigration from other parts of the world, particularly Europe. Thus, a colonial connection exists, but most of the developments can be subsumed into other concepts, such as the world economy.

The American Revolution warrants more attention because it helps to illustrate the range and trajectories of the Atlantic revolutions. The American Revolution undoubtedly inspired revolutionary activities in Western Europe, particularly in France, and provided inspiration to the Latin American wars of independence. This moment in U.S. history must be addressed in world history, along with a number of other examples.

During the early-19th century, the United States was preoccupied with domestic developments and westward expansion, which brought the nation into further contact with Canada and Mexico. The United States was also preoccupied with defining American institutions and characteristics and addressing the slave issue. These developments are important, but they do not necessarily require extensive treatment from a world history standpoint.

By the time we reach the 1860s or the post–Civil War period, we must treat the United States as a significant part of world history. By this point, the U.S. economy, although still dependent on European capital and technological inspiration, had grown sufficiently to influence world trade patterns. The United States also became involved in global arms trade, a theme that remains consistent in world history to the present day. The United States was a somewhat conflicted imperial power, taking important colonies in the 1890s but also criticizing colonial activity. In the early-20th century, the United States became involved in the course of European diplomacy, playing intermediary between European combatants and, with World War I, directly entering the diplomatic-military mainstream. We see a brief pullback with isolationism, but from the final third of the 19th century to the present, the United States is a prime actor in world affairs.

What analytical framework do we use to place the United States in the world history context? In these lectures, we have frequently used the civilizational approach, looking at particular societies to make sense of comparative developments and larger world forces. Is the United States a separate civilization or not? If not, the usual alternative would be to treat the United States as part of an expanded Western civilization zone. A legitimate case can be made for treating the United States as a separate civilization. This is the thrust of the American exceptionalist argument, but there is an alternative argument.

The United States can be fit into a smaller number of *settler societies* that emerged in the 18th and 19th centuries. Settler societies are those in which the majority of the population is European but which also encompass native peoples and other strands of immigration; settler societies are also frontier societies. The United States might be viewed as the most important case of a larger nexus of settler societies that includes Canada, Australia, and New Zealand.

Returning to the question of whether the United States constitutes its own civilization, what durable and distinctive characteristics can we find to make that case? In contrast to Western civilization until the 20th century, the United States never had a true aristocracy or a peasantry; the free farming tradition of the United States differs markedly in terms of economic behavior and political impulses.

The United States also had an experience of internal slavery and, following slavery, racial issues that did not affect Western civilization to the same degree. It has frequently experienced levels of crime, particularly violent crime, much different from those of Western Europe. In contrast to Western Europe, the United States managed to industrialize and modernize while remaining on the whole an intensely religious society. It also has been much more hostile to socialism than Western Europe and has never developed a significant welfare state by European standards. The idea of the United States as a nation of more inventive people compared to Europeans or others has largely faded away. The notion that the United States offers more social mobility than other parts of the world is not borne out by the data, although it is interesting that Americans believe their society to be more open.

We can legitimately point to some distinctive American features, but we need to balance this with the recognition that the United States continues to share much with a larger Western zone. For example, American industrialization in the early-19th century proceeded almost as part of the same process of industrialization that affected France, Belgium, Germany, and elsewhere. In the same period, the United States began to reduce its birth rate; this occurred at the same basic time and for the same basic reasons as in many West European countries. The reentry of married women into the labor force of the 1950s and 1960s was essentially the same phenomenon for the United States and Western Europe; the sexual revolution that began around 1960 also had the same pattern in both places.

As we try to place the United States in a world history context, we must recognize these issues relating to categorization and civilizational framework. We should also note that relationships between the United States and Western Europe have not remained constant. In the decades immediately after World War II, the United States and Western Europe seem to converge, but recent decades have seen increased separation.

As the United States becomes more important in world affairs, does it exert a special mark on the rest of the world or does it follow a dynamic already established by larger Western interactions? Without question, the United States exercises increasing power and has increasing influence on world events in the contemporary period. But in doing so, has the nation become more significant?

The United States was not the origin of modern consumer society; Western Europe was, as we've touched on previously. But the United States embraced consumerism increasingly in the 19th century.

Europeans frequently argue that as the United States became more important in world affairs the nation displayed a combination of inexperience and moralistic naiveté that contrasted with the more sober, realistic approach that Europeans took. Some critics have argued that the United States displays an unusual pension for high-tech approaches to military activities, particularly in World War II and the years afterward. Analysts have argued that the United States became more interested than Western Europe in promoting the destruction of colonialism and encouraging democracy.

And a case can be made for American influence in shaping world consumerism: the United States was not the origin of modern consumerist society, but it embraced consumerism and played a significant popular cultural role in world affairs.

We must note that as the United States became more potent in world affairs, it assumed the neo-imperialist mantle that Western Europe had developed: it tried to pick up pieces of empire, for example, from the French and Vietnam or pieces of British policy in the Middle East and Greece after World War II.

The same idea applies to its core activities: in its interest to obtain access to cheap goods and protect export opportunities for high-tech operations and basic food stuffs, the United States behaves much as core societies have since the advent of the world economy.

The debate about the place of the United States in world history is a difficult and revealing one, in which historical traditions play against contemporary operations and the United States can be seen as both a separate civilization and part of a larger Western thrust. ■

Suggested Reading

Michael Adas, *Dominance by Design: Technological Imperatives and America's Civilizing Mission*.

Carl Guarneri, ed., *America Compared: American History in International Perspective Since 1865*.

Seymour Martin Lipset, *American Exceptionalism: A Double-Edged Sword*.

Charles Maier, *Among Empires: American Ascendancy and Its Predecessors*.

Questions to Consider

1. Is the United States a separate civilization with crucial exceptions to Western patterns, or should it be considered Western with a few special twists?

2. Why was the United States positioned to become such a leader in global consumerism?

Contemporary Democracy
Lecture 33

Our discussion today focuses on political change in the contemporary period of world history and, more specifically, on the various surges and, sometimes, setbacks of political democracy.

I n 1900, most of the world's political systems revolved around monarchy, empire, and colony. These highly traditional political forms would steadily erode in the 20th century, as monarchy proved unsatisfactory (save perhaps at the figurehead level) in all but a few regions, colonies fell victim to nationalism, and multinational empires proved difficult to sustain. In place of these forms, three main political configurations emerged. Totalitarian systems, whether communist or fascist, were one option; authoritarian regimes—less systematic in their use of power than the totalitarians, though equally intolerant of political competition—were another; and democracies were a third.

As the contemporary period of world history opened, democracy seemed to be spreading from its base in Western Europe, the United States, and Australia. But its spread in Central and East-Central Europe and in southern Europe proved short-lived, Mexico moved to a one-party model, and Japan's strides toward democracy were undercut by military authoritarians. As is well known, the 1930s were not kind to the democratic system of government; some advance occurred as a result of World War II in the defeated Axis powers but most strikingly in India; on the other hand, most new nations, though often launched as democracies, quickly retreated toward authoritarianism.

A wider pattern opened in the 1970s, with changes in southern Europe and, particularly, Latin America. Democracy reached new parts of Asia in the 1980s, and of course, changes in the Soviet Empire created still further opportunities. Democracies spread more widely in Africa in the 1990s and reached a discussion stage in the Middle East early in the 21st century. At the same time, however, there were some new question marks as liberal democracy receded in Russia. The fact remains that by the early-21st century, democracy was more widespread than ever before in world history. What factors supported it? Key holdouts, such as China and much of the Middle East, also raise questions: Why did they stand apart? Was their resistance likely to change? Would some form of democracy (not necessarily exactly the Western model) prove the norm for governments in this most recent period of world history?

We will begin with a definition of democracy as a system that gives the majority of people opportunities to vote for political candidates and political parties. Also part of democracy are opportunities for reasonable freedom of expression and for different candidates and different parties to compete in elections. In the 20th and 21st centuries, the United States has periodically been a sponsor of democracy in other parts of the world.

By the early-21st century, almost no part of the world had the same system of government as it had a century before. The dominant political forms of the early-20th century were empires and monarchies. Empires fell because they could not sustain themselves against the rising tide of nationalism and demands for independence; this was the fate of the European colonial empires, Austria-Hungary, the Ottoman Empire, and later, elements of the Russian Empire. Monarchies fell and were replaced with republics because they were not supple enough to fit modern circumstances. In some instances, monarchies fell victim to their association with aristocratic and agricultural social systems.

No uniform pattern of response emerged to political change in the contemporary period. Fascist totalitarian regimes emerged in the 1920s–1930s. Fascism appealed in societies that faced significant national frustration, defeat in war, or appetites for more territory. Fascism emerged where there were pronounced social divisions, often serving as a popular cover for upper-class domination. Fascism served as a vehicle for leadership ambitions and for efforts to use propaganda and intimidation to link peoples with this new principle of leadership.

Totalitarianism involved governments that sought to control most aspects of society and to eliminate all vigorous forms of political opposition. Communist totalitarian options emerged in societies that were seized by communist revolutions or conquered by communist regimes. Communism is not the same as fascism or totalitarianism, but it coincided with fascism in its emphasis on strong central government control, efforts to appeal to popular support, and insistence on active popular loyalty.

In an updated version of authoritarianism, leaders, political parties, or military forces seize control of a society and seek to eliminate political opposition. They do not, however, construct quite such a powerful central government apparatus as fascism or communism. Authoritarianism surfaced in countries where social divisions ran deep, and agreement on any single political or social system without imposing authoritarian controls was difficult. Such controls also surfaced in some societies that were eager to modernize but mistrustful of other mechanisms for doing so.

Contemporary world history began with World War I. The aftermath of World War I initially seemed somewhat encouraging to possibilities for the spread of democracy to areas of the world beyond its then-current home in Western society. The Mexican revolution flirted with democratic systems and installed universal suffrage but fairly quickly turned to a reduction of political competition in favor of one-party rule.

Democracy was established in Germany and Italy for the first time and in most of the new regimes of East-Central Europe. Most of these regimes were incapable of sustaining democracy, given the inexperience of their citizenry with democratic forms and the social divisions within these regions. In East-Central Europe, for example, sharp divisions existed between landlords and peasants, such that landlords supported authoritarian alternatives as a means to inhibit social unrest. The only durable democracy to emerge from this East-Central European zone in the interwar period was that of Czechoslovakia.

Democratic systems were briefly installed in Japan in the early 1920s, but these too quickly fell victim to more authoritarian leadership and the demands of military authorities. The surge of democracy suggested that the success of this system in some parts of the West provided a logical model for many new regimes. Nonetheless, the interwar period is not dominated by the durable spread of democracy. Democracy even faltered in its home base of Western Europe, where the erosion of centralist parties, increasing social conflicts, and divisions over responses to fascist and communist threats paralyzed many democracies.

The aftermath of the Second World War ushered in a more durable expansion of democracy beyond its previous concentration in North America and Western Europe. Noteworthy was the establishment of democracy in Western Germany and Italy under Allied occupation and in Japan. Soon after World War II, a democratic government was established in India, newly independent from the British. In the decades immediately after World War II, new nations' issues—lack of experienced leadership, lack of citizen experience with democracy, disputes over boundaries, disputes over social systems, and internal social strife—tended to yield fairly quick replacement of initial democratic experiments with authoritarian leadership.

Beginning in the 1970s, a new current can be discerned that seems to lead fairly directly to the present-day pattern of an unusually extensive hold of democratic systems in the world at large. The 1970s saw the establishment of democratic systems in the southern fringes of Europe, Spain, Portugal, and Greece, where monarchies and/or authoritarian systems had previously flourished. From the late 1970s to the 1990s, virtually every Latin American country except Cuba would embrace democratic systems. The 1980s saw democracies installed in a number of places in East and Southeast Asia, usually on the heels of popular agitation.

Democratic systems also began to develop from the mid-1980s to the early 1990s in most parts of what had been the former Soviet Empire. Gorbachev's decision in 1985 to open Russia to new levels of political discussion and competition led in the direction of a multiparty democratic system. The dismantling of the Soviet Empire resulted in a number of democratic installations in almost all former Soviet or Soviet-dominated territory in East-Central Europe and in some other parts of the former Soviet Empire.

The 1990s saw the expansion of democracy in many parts of sub-Saharan Africa. Crucial here were the establishment of democracy in Nigeria and the dismantling of apartheid and the establishment of a successful political system in South Africa. Early in the 21st century, additional democracies were established in such places as Ukraine, Georgia, and Indonesia.

The causes for this spread are fairly easy to determine. The spread of democracy was encouraged by the Western powers and, to some degree, Japan and India. The Western powers' interest in spreading democracy stemmed partly from Cold War competitions and partly from a genuine commitment to democracy as the preferred political form. The spread of democracy in Latin America in the late 1970s owed a good bit to U.S. foreign policy under President Carter. By the 1970s and 1980s, the West was sufficiently out of the game of defending imperialism that societies could emulate its model without the sense that they were caving in to imperialist control.

Democratic political systems also spread because of the wide belief in a direct association between democracy and economic prosperity. Many Latin American systems converted because of a belief that democracy would bring an added commitment to freer enterprise and a dismantling of former state interventions in the economy. Gorbachev's opening of the Russian political system was directly tied to his deep commitment to economic reform. By the late 1980s, the failure of the Marxist political alternative meant that people interested in political change had a smaller set of options available to them.

The democratic surge has still not taken hold in key parts of the world. China's decision in 1978 to introduce market reforms was accompanied by an equally clear assertion that the authoritarian aspect of communist political rule would not budge.

The Middle East is another region in which democracy remains the exception rather than the rule, although there are a few stirrings in the early-21st century, partly under American encouragement. Israel, at least for Israeli citizens, is a democratic beacon. By the late-20th century, Turkey was fairly firmly established in the camp of durable democratic countries. Much of the Middle East, however, remains anchored in one-party systems, authoritarian rule, and monarchy.

China and many parts of the Middle East raise issues concerning the interaction between older traditions and more recent developments. China offers an interesting combination of an undemocratic Confucian tradition and a relatively recent revolution whose aftermath may still be inhibiting the growth of democracy. We see a similar case in the Middle East, with the combination of Islamic traditions and the fall of the Ottoman Empire in the early-20th century, and the formation of a new group of nations.

What is clear, again, is that political change has been a key feature of the contemporary period of world history.

The other main issue in the spread of democracy in the late-20th century and early 21st involves durability. By the early 21st century, authoritarian impulses seemed to be gaining ascendancy among Russian leadership. In a few Latin American instances, questions arose about whether societies that have not previously sustained long periods of democratic rule would be able to do so now.

Other factors might encourage greater optimism for democracy. As the use of computers proliferated, for example, experts wondered whether this technological underpinning might see democracy spread still further.

Political change has been a key feature of the contemporary period and has yielded an unprecedented interest in democratic political forms. The contemporary period, however, has produced a variety of political impulses. The early-21st century saw a wave of socialist victories in Latin American elections. The same thing may occur as democracies spread to other parts of the world, particularly the Middle East. The spread of democracy does not necessarily erase the need to pay ongoing attention to global political complexity. ■

Suggested Reading

Ben Eklof, *Soviet Briefing: Gorbachev and the Reform Period*.

Francis Fukayama, *The End of History and the Last Man*.

C. J. Fuller and Veronique Benei, *The Everyday State and Society in Modern India*.

Peter H. Smith, *Democracy in Latin America: Political Change in Comparative Perspective.*

1. Why was democracy more successful, worldwide, at the end of the 20th century than it was during the century's first five decades?

2. Given the reasons for democracy's global spread and for China's insistence on an alternative, what are the prospects for a Chinese turn to democracy in the near future?

Contemporary Cultural Change
Lecture 34

The contemporary period of world history has seen massive amounts of cultural change in most parts of the world. In this sense, the contemporary period might be compared to the postclassical period as a time in which large numbers of people rethought or were encouraged to rethink many aspects of their traditional beliefs.

There were also connections between cultural and political change. Several factors pushed for cultural change: new levels of contact among societies (including the impact of returning immigrants), rapid urbanization, and active "missionary" activity by leaders eager to convey new political attachments or simply to sell consumer goods. It is also clear that directions of change were complex and a great deal of resistance developed, particularly from the 1970s onward. Even more than change, then, cultural contest both among and within societies describes the contemporary period to date.

Three ideologies gained ground, particularly during the first three quarters of the 20th century and often at the expense of traditional religious beliefs: nationalism, Marxism, and liberal humanitarianism. These three belief systems were quite different, and are often opposed in principle though open to combination in practice. They also shared key features. They were secular, they pointed to progress on this Earth, and they usually urged a new level of faith in science.

But there were other cultural claimants as well, particularly among religions. In Africa, for example, the spread of Christianity and Islam defined the most important cultural changes, though consumerism and nationalism also spread to a degree. Latin America saw a variety of new religious enthusiasms, most recently, Protestant evangelicalism. More important still, the rise of religious fundamentalisms from the 1970s onward added tremendous complexity to the world's cultural map, dividing loyalties within such regions as India, the United States, and the Middle East and sometimes dividing loyalties within families or individuals.

The contemporary period has seen massive cultural change in most parts of the world. In this sense, it might be compared to the postclassical period.

If we look at the dominant cultural systems of most parts of the world around 1900, we see the continued hold of the world religions. If we fast-forward to a century later, the hold of the religions has been qualified, and the cultural map quite has become more complex. Although there was no global agreement on a new political system, there was wide agreement that the old systems no longer worked. The same is not true for culture. In this arena, we see significant cultural contestation and competition within and among regions and even within individuals.

There are several reasons to see the contemporary period in terms of cultural change, including new migration patterns, massive urbanization, and active "missionary" efforts for one or more new kinds of beliefs. In addition, each of the revolutions of the contemporary period attacked older cultural systems in favor of new commitments.

Three main competitors emerged for cultural allegiance in the contemporary period, none of which was entirely new. The first entrant was nationalism. As we saw earlier, nationalism praised tradition to some extent and could combine with older belief systems. Nationalism, however, tended to move people at least partially away from older religious formulations. Indian nationalism urged Indians to retain their older commitments to Hinduism or Islam but to modify these with new views about social castes and class, gender, and politics. African nationalists attacked older polytheistic religious loyalties and introduced important social and political divisions.

The most systematic competitor for cultural allegiance in the 20th century was Marxism, which has some elements of religion. Marxism argues that religion is explicitly wrong and that people should free themselves of it in preparation for the revolution. Marxism urges attention to scientific principles of history and to science itself, along with a commitment to materialism and the material forces that drive the historical process. Marxism urges commitment to principles of social equality and to new political formulations. In the hands of leaders in the 20th century, Marxism produced not only beliefs but also martyrs, symbols, and rituals deliberately designed to compete with older religious forms.

The third competitor for belief in the contemporary period has been called by anthropologists *liberal humanitarianism*. This belief system emphasizes three principal identities or commitments. The first of these is consumerism, a cultural system in which people gain part of their satisfaction and part of their personal and group identities from the process of consuming goods that they do not necessarily need. Liberal humanitarianism involves a substantial commitment to science as a means of explaining the world around us and as the potential solution for many social and individual ills. Liberal humanitarianism involves a considerable degree of tolerance and cosmopolitanism, as well as a sense that other people and cultures offer opportunities for learning.

In challenging traditional beliefs, these three systems frequently challenged each other. Marx and Marxists leaders described nationalism as another cultural component that could mislead the working classes. Nationalists were frequently hostile to consumerism as an individualistic form of expression.

Despite their differences, these systems also combined with one another and with older cultural values: for example, many Japanese consumerists, living in a society that was increasingly secular, continued to use some Buddhist rituals, and male Italian Marxists often had their children baptized—just in case.

These three belief systems shared some points in common. The three systems were secular. They all judged society and individuals in terms of activities in this world. The three systems were also, broadly speaking, progressive; they believed that society, over time, would become better if the national state gained ground, as the communist revolution took hold, or as standards of living rose. These belief systems tended to emphasize the goal of the individual to find greater satisfaction in this life rather than in the afterlife.

These systems had some commitment to science. Marx prided himself on the scientific qualities of his theories. Most nationalists urged attention to science to increase national strength. These cultural packages challenged the primary cultural identifiers of the world in 1900, but they have not yet dislodged older beliefs as clearly as new political systems dislodged their older counterparts.

These cultural packages do not fit some key regions, most notably, sub-Saharan Africa. This region has been the scene of massive cultural change in the contemporary period, with elements of Marxism, nationalism, and liberal humanitarianism. But the big cultural story in 20th-century sub-Saharan Africa has been the massive gains of Islam and Christianity among the populace. Latin America has also seen some interest in nationalism, Marxism, and liberal humanitarianism, but much of the cultural story of Latin America in the past half century has been the increasing interest in Protestant fundamentalism. In the wake of the fall of Marxism in Eastern Europe and the reduction of Marxist cultural enthusiasm, people are once again open to new religious influences in both Russia and China.

A significant issue relating to these cultural belief systems involves the rise of religious fundamentalism, not only in Islam, but also in Western Christianity, Hinduism, Judaism, and Buddhism. Religious fundamentalism urges the transcendent importance of religious commitments and a religious cultural framework over the new forces of nationalism, Marxism, or liberal humanitarianism.

Religious fundamentalists urge a return to an established body of religious truth, often involving strict moral codes and rearrangements of gender relationships. Religious fundamentalism typically involves innovation; fundamentalists are adept at using technological devices to spread their message and win adherence. Many religions, under the spur of fundamentalism, become more intolerant than they had been traditionally. Many fundamentalists insist increasingly on the importance of gaining state support for their religious goals and beliefs. The rise of fundamentalism indicates a definite reaction to secular cultural alternatives and a reaction to the somewhat more tolerant approaches within a religion itself; it further suggests innovation, particularly in political policy and the uses of technology.

Why is fundamentalism gaining ground? Fundamentalism is a reassertion of real or imagined traditional identity against the cosmopolitan features of new cultural systems. Religious revivals reflect the fact that many of the new cultural systems fail to provide spiritual satisfaction. Religious fundamentalism has frequently appealed to social groups who find themselves left out of the benefits, real or imagined, of the modern world. The cultural collapse of Marxism may also be a factor.

What are the results of these changes in cultural belief systems? One result is a certain degree of regional division. A few regions, such as Western Europe, seem largely content to remain secular; their cultural change has reached a fairly uniform conclusion. Most parts of the world, however, have seen internal divisions and conflict among groups within the region. We see such conflict between secular loyalties and leadership and religious enthusiasms in the Middle East, the United States, Latin America, and to some degree Africa.

We do not know the end of the story of cultural change; we can, however, note the complexity that cultural divisions within and among regions add to the story of global politics and the future of world history. ■

Suggested Reading

Gurdas Ahuja, *BJP and Indian Politics: Policies and Programmes of the Bharatiya Janata Party.*

Richard Antoun, *Understanding Fundamentalism.*

Dilip Hiro, *Holy Wars: The Rise of Islamic Fundamentalism.*

Questions to Consider

1. What were the main similarities and what were the main differences between Marxist culture and the cultures of consumer societies? What major factors supported the spread of each of these cultural systems?

2. What explains the rise of religious fundamentalisms? What is the most satisfactory definition of fundamentalism, and why do some scholars reject the term as an oversimplification? What was new about fundamentalisms compared to traditional religions?

Gender in Contemporary World History
Lecture 35

Changes in gender relations and debates and questions about gender relations constitute one of the really important themes in the contemporary period of world history.

The contemporary period of world history is a crucial point of change in gender relations and conditions for women. In turn, gender issues form part of the definition of this period after many centuries in which no fundamental developments occurred in this arena at a global level. At the same time, questions must be raised about the uniformity and extent of change, which makes gender history a complex part of the contemporary global mosaic. Though there were differences in timing and extent, widespread changes occurred in women's educational access and in key political and legal rights.

Many of these developments were supported by international nongovernmental organizations and, after 1945, by the United Nations. Changes in work roles occurred, but there was great variety here, depending on region and location. Widespread reductions in birthrates also affected gender relations. At the same time, many formal and informal forces were eager to maintain more traditional gender roles.

We will begin with some background to our discussion of gender issues. Patriarchal gender relations were characteristic of agricultural economies. We also saw that the classical civilizations enshrined patriarchal relationships in codes of law and conduct.

In the postclassical period, two contradictory trends emerged that constituted the next reshaping of gender relationships. The spread of world religions established a degree of spiritual equality between men and women and began to attack certain traditional practices, such as female infanticide. Some trends were established that could worsen women's conditions, such as the practice of foot-binding in China.

Neither the early modern period nor the Long 19th Century introduced systematic global changes in gender relations, although there were specific social and regional developments. The contemporary period ushered in some developments that clearly erode traditional patriarchy, although they do not necessarily establish true equality. This period of world history will probably be regarded as one in which many traditional gender assumptions were rethought and traditional relationships reconstituted.

A number of factors pushed for change in the contemporary period. Most of the revolutions of the 20th century, in contrast to the Atlantic revolutions, did not have real gender impact, although most of these revolutions heralded their implications for gender relations. Except in Iran, women found in the revolutionary regimes new opportunities for public roles; principles of legal equality were also established. The fact of rhetorical change itself and the changes in opportunities for women were significant. Nationalist movements often used women actively then shunted them aside, but the process of galvanizing women to voice their concerns helped to accelerate change.

World economic relationships also had an impact on gender. Changes in production processes provided new opportunities for women—for example, in certain kinds of factories—but they also produced new competition for women's work. Larger processes, such as urbanization and the reduction of infant mortality, had an impact on women.

Increasingly important from the 1950s onward were the operations of governmental and nongovernmental international agencies. By the late-19th century, a number of international feminist movements had formed that pressed a women's rights agenda on governments and international agencies around the world. The U.N. Charter Statements of Rights conventionally included gender issues and provided a framework for pressure in individual societies toward changing gender laws and gender relationships more widely. In 1965, the United Nations began to sponsor a "Year of the Woman" every decade or even a "Decade of the Woman." The U.N. conferences also spawned local nongovernmental organizations (NGOs) to work on women's right issues and report on these issues to larger groups such as Amnesty International.

During the 20th and early-21st centuries, change took certain clear directions. Beginning a little before World War I in Scandinavia and after the war in the United States, the Soviet Union, Germany, Turkey, and other European countries, voting rights for women were established. Other legal rights were attached to this basic conversion in suffrage systems, including divorce and property rights.

In education, women gained ground during the 2^{0th} and, to date, the 21st centuries. By the early-21st century, in an impressive variety of societies, women began to gain majority ascendancy even in higher education. Parity in education could be expected to translate into greater job opportunities and political voice.

Voting rights, legal rights, and educational change propelled increasing female representation in elected legislatures. Gains have been made in this area in the United States, Europe, South Asia, China, and Russia. Women also gained a new measure of equality in consumerism, participating in opportunities to buy things as a means of self-expression.

As women do gain new opportunities for expression and new levels of education, they may continue to differ regionally in terms of the goals they seek.

These changes applied to almost every region of the world and brought an end to literal patriarchal systems. Feminists still use the term "patriarchy" as a means of pointing out inequalities, but from a historical standpoint, developments in the 20th century suggest the beginning of the end of patriarchal systems that had predominated through the long agricultural period of world history. Not all the systems work the way they are supposed to. In rural India, for example, women have the right to vote, but fathers or husbands check to make sure they vote "correctly."

In gender relations, as in so many aspects of contemporary world history, we can point to patterns of change, new issues, and new causes, but we do not know the end of the story. We can also highlight intriguing complexities. Some regions have more smoothly adopted gender change than others.

Regions that have experienced revolution, such as China, see far less debate about new roles for women than do regions where change has been more incremental, such as rural India or the Middle East.

By the end of the 20th century, every major region in the world was participating in a slowing of the birthrate. Some regions had achieved what's known as the demographic transition, in which the average woman has a small number of children, almost all of whom live. Western Europe and the United States experienced demographic transitions by the end of the 19th century or the early-20th, while Japan and the Soviet Union did so either between the World Wars or right after World War II. Latin America experienced its demographic transition in the 1970s.

Sub-Saharan Africa and some Islamic regions have yet to experience a demographic transition, even though their birthrates have begun to drop. We do not know for sure whether succeeding decades will demonstrate that this is another area where women's conditions are changing in similar directions. This tendency to reduce the birthrate will inevitably have additional implications for women's lives and their relationships with men in the future.

Along with new rights and increased access to education have come new opportunities for or new demands on women to participate in the labor force outside the home. Communist societies usually insisted on substantial levels of work for women, although women might be paid less than men and have limited opportunities in certain occupations. In Western Europe and the United States, women's work commitments gained ground systematically only from the later 1950s onward. Japan entered this picture a little later and seems to be moving in a similar direction.

Some of the more exploited areas of the world economy seemed to discourage women's work participation: in Africa, for example, as peripheral-type jobs expanded, men tended to seize them and leave the women responsible for agriculture. Similar developments occurred with the fall of communism and Marxism in much of Eastern Europe: with the loss of Marxism's support for gender equality and with increasing economic turmoil, many women found their economic positions eroding.

Individual men and groups of men in many societies have found ways to retaliate against women for the gains they have achieved. It is likely that violence against women has increased in contemporary world history, with men using direct attacks on women as a way to express their frustration and as a reaction to pressures urging revisions of traditional gender relationships. It is also possible that rape and violence against women have increased as instruments of war. Sometimes the "pushback" of men may take legal form as in the revival of customary legal codes.

Western feminists and other advocates, until recently, have usually agreed on a human rights agenda for women, but some are now arguing that the Western version of feminism is not what they want. Some Indian women, for example, have written that they do not want to see arranged marriages replaced with Western marriage patterns. Arranged marriages are seen as better for women and more likely to be stable and put less pressure on women to beautify themselves for men.

Many Middle Eastern women may wish to revise Islam to some extent but without adopting a Western version of women's rights. In Egypt and elsewhere, veiling is seen by some women as an important expression of their ability to make individual choices and a gesture of defiance against undue international influences.

Some African feminists have argued that the Western international women's rights package is too individualistic and that Africa has its own traditions of collective and family protection for women. These complex gender issues remain a fundamental part of the shaping of the contemporary period in world history. ■

Suggested Reading

N. Berkovitch, *From Motherhood to Citizenship: Women's Rights and International Organizations*.

Elizabeth Croll, *Feminism and Socialism in China*.

B. J. Nelson and Najma Chowdhury eds., *Women and Politics Worldwide*.

1. Why were Western gender standards so influential in global discussions during the contemporary period of world history?

2. Adding up the main changes and discussions concerning women since the 1920s and granting continued variations and inequalities, is the patriarchal system of gender relations, so long dominant in world history, on the way out? Is it possible to define the system that will replace it?

Globalization and World History
Lecture 36

The most exciting social science concept to hit the streets in the 1990s was the concept of globalization, focusing obviously on intensification of contacts among various societies in the world to the extent that basic frameworks of life were set by these contacts.

Globalization gives us an opportunity to look at the sweep of world history in terms of key moments and issues as a means of setting this phenomenon in an appropriate historical context. The idea of globalization became a hot theory in Western social science circles in the 1990s. Much discussion focused on whether the process was a good thing or not, with fairly extreme positions taken on both sides. The general sense, however, was that globalization was producing a very different world from periods past; a group calling themselves new global historians has amplified this claim.

Figuring out how dramatic globalization is raises some challenging issues. Assessment is further complicated by resistance to globalization. Two or three historical models are worth considering. In addition, different aspects of globalization can be assessed, breaking down what is sometimes presented as a single package. The subject is sweeping and can seem rather abstract, but it relates to some very specific developments.

For example, the United Arab Emirates ban on using young boys as riders in camel races in 2004 influenced the 2005 U.S. Supreme Court ruling that minors should not be subject to the death penalty, after years in which the United States and Somalia had been the only countries to resist an international convention on this subject. Why the long holdout and why the change? Globalization touches a wide variety of policies and behaviors and, by definition, a wide swathe of geography.

We will begin by further defining globalization. Globalization depends on rapid technological changes, particularly in communication and transportation. New connective technologies form a basic part of the definition of the 20th century as a new period in world history. Globalization also involves a wide range of activity. In 2004, the United Arab Emirates banned the use of boy jockeys in camel races because leaders realized that world opinion would disapprove of this use of children. A year later, the U.S. Supreme Court ruled that children could not be put to death for crimes, specifically citing the importance of world opinion in setting standards for the nation. Globalization represents a certain optimism for the future, although this idea can be taken to extremes.

Throughout this course, we have seen a recurrent tension between human interest in forming local and regional societies with established identities and the advantages or inescapability of contacts with other societies. This tension has been progressively redefined throughout history; in one way, globalization is simply the latest iteration of this redefinition. Even at the time of agriculture and early civilizations, aspects of globalization were already emerging. People began migrating early, and migration is still a key feature of globalization, although now it can take place more quickly and over longer distances and it involves the possibility of return. The spread of disease, another key aspect of globalization, also has early roots that have changed with globalization. The globalization phenomenon allows disease to spread more rapidly but also has spawned such institutions as the World Health Organization.

In the early stages of the human experience, contacts formed a vital but subordinate theme; the attention of leaders and ordinary people alike was devoted to the formation of local and regional societies, clusters of institutions, and clusters of cultural identities. In the classical period we saw a system of contacts that connected the various classical societies from China to Rome along such routes as the great Silk Road. We also noted, however, that at this point, the balance between regional focus and interregional contact was still slanted in favor of the regional.

With the postclassical period, we saw the balance shift decisively. Some world historians would argue that what we now call globalization actually began around 1000 C.E. During this era, trade among various regions in Afro-Eurasia routinely and fundamentally connected various societies. From about 1000 C.E. onward, many world historians see an intensification of this basic framework, rooted in trade, that would make contacts and convergences superior to regional identities. With the addition of the Americas and Oceania to the list of societies involved in global contacts and with the intensification of trade and biological connections, the early modern period is another chapter in this ongoing intensification.

With the postclassical era, some world historians would argue that the framework for globalization was already established. In discussing the phenomenon today, we need only note subsequent intensification in patterns of interaction and dependence on contact. Alternatives to this view, however, argue for greater change in the last one or two centuries.

Many historians now argue that the process of globalization, as distinct from earlier patterns of contact, began in the Long 19th Century. In this period, we see new technology and other developments that helped link societies more rapidly than before and intensified international trade. In the Long 19th Century, we also see the first signs of what we now call cultural globalization. At the end of the 19th century, for example, international interest in sports emerged, which would be a key element of international culture from that point onward.

In the Long 19th Century, we see the early phases of political globalization with, for example, agreements relating to international mail and the treatment of prisoners of war.

The 20th century raises several issues in connection with globalization. In the second quarter of the 20th century, a number of societies deliberately pulled away from globalization. This reaction against globalization, which was not yet seen as acceptable, strengthens the argument that this phenomenon began in the late-19th century. By the second half of the 20th century, new organizational capacity, particularly in the form of multinational corporations, offered a way to measure 20th-century globalization as a partially new phenomenon.

Also in the 20th century, environmental change and anti-globalization protests were added to the picture. In the 19th century and earlier, human activities mainly had regional environmental consequences; in the later-20th century, people realized that activities in one region can have an environmental impact on distant regions. The first explicit protests against globalization began in 1999. This was a sign that globalization had become sufficiently defined as a force against which groups with particular interests could unite.

The 20th and 21st centuries can be seen as different from the Long 19th Century in the extent of technological change and the implications of various aspects of global contact. These two themes may finally convince people that the 20th and 21st centuries embody the crucial measures of globalization. Globalization almost inevitably must be viewed in the larger lens of world history, forcing us to look back to previous types of contact and previous concerns about contact. This broader vision enables us to see what is new and recapitulative about the globalization process.

The broad view is crucial in assessing the quality of globalization. Do economic advantages outweigh the costs to specific cultural identities? Do economic advantages spread widely or uniformly enough? These questions take on new meaning with the world historical view. World history also contributes greater understanding of the extent to which different societies, because of their prior historical experience and cultural and institutional contexts, respond differently to common forces of change, including globalization. Globalization is a process that rouses resistance and accommodation. In the Middle East, Europe, and the United States, we see a significant accommodation to globalization, but we also see concerns about religion, migration, and issues of political sovereignty in relation to globalization.

> **World history, in a sense—intriguing, I hope, in its own right—is a vital tool to help us sort out what shapes our present and what will shape our future.**

Just as world history provides a perspective on globalization, so, too, does globalization provide an opportunity to renew our sense of why the world history enterprise is a significant one. There are many good reasons to be interested in history, among them, the opportunity to see how the past shapes the present. Given that our present is inescapably a global one, world history is a crucial framework for understanding our own times. Contacts are not a new phenomenon, nor is resistance to contact; in the 19th century and, perhaps, again in the later-20th century, however, this basic tension between the regional and the global changed crucially. World history helps us make that determination. World history is also essential in helping us to determine why different societies react to globalization in different ways and in helping us sort out the impact of globalization on our own society and others.

In these lectures, we have argued that since about 3500 B.C.E., the concept of civilization is one of the key mechanisms by which we can make sense of the variety of experiences that constitute world history. We have also argued that civilization is a form of human organization, but that as individual civilizations developed, they formed identities and characteristics that would mark them off, in part, from other societies.

By the 21st century, under the impact of globalization, are we reaching a point at which civilization itself—as an expression of identity—will begin to yield ground to other, more global forms of identity? If the answer to this question is yes, we would seem to be in an era that is experiencing a fundamental shift away from some of the common currency that world history has maintained for more than 5,000 years.

Some historians argue that civilization will trump globalization, and we will see a clash of civilizations focused particularly on tensions between Islam and the West. We do not know the future, but we do know that we cannot even formulate sensible questions or examine possibilities without knowing the history that lies at their base. World history is a vital tool to help us sort out what shapes our present and what will shape our future. ∎

Suggested Reading

John Gray, *False Dawn: The Delusions of Global Capitalism*.

Ramachandra Guha, *Environmentalism: A Global History*.

Bruce Mazlish, *The New Global History*.

1. Who wins and who loses under globalization?

2. What is the best overall argument, with appropriate evidence, for seeing globalization as a very new phenomenon?

Timeline

Prehistoric Landmarks

c. 2–2.5 million
years ago ....More humanlike species with larger brain size in
eastern Africa.

120,000 years ago ....Arrival of Homo sapiens sapiens; later
displacement of Neanderthals and other species
across Asia and Europe from initial center
in Africa.

25,000 B.C.E.....................Passage of people to the Americas via land link
from Asia.

8000–5000 B.C.E.............Further improvements in tool making; first
development of agriculture; great expansion in
human population.

4000–3500 B.C.E.............Early use of bronze and copper tools.

1500 B.C.E.......................Early use of iron tools and weapons.

River Valley Civilizations

3500–2600 B.C.E.............Sumerian kingdom, development of cuneiform
writing; river valley civilizations also in Egypt
and India.

1150–130 B.C.E...............Books of the Jewish Old Testament written.

Classical Civilizations

China

1029–258 B.C.E...............China's Zhou dynasty.

551–478 B.C.E.................Confucius.

202 B.C.E.–220 C.E.........Han dynasty.

India

c. 563–483 B.C.E. .... Gautama Buddha.

322–184 B.C.E. .... Mauryan dynasty.

Mediterranean (Greece and Rome)

800 B.C.E. .... Rise of Greek city-states and economy; Homeric epics, Iliad and Odyssey; beginnings of Rome.

330 B.C.E. ff .... Macedonian Empire; Alexander the Great.

27 B.C.E. .... Augustus Caesar; rise of Roman Empire; 476, fall of Rome.

313 C.E. .... Constantine adopts Christianity.

The Extension of Civilization

Middle East

570–632 .... Muhammad and the foundation of Islam.

750–1258 .... Abbasid caliphate.

Western Europe

800–814 .... Charlemagne's empire.

Americas

1350 ff. .... Formation of Aztec Empire; height of Incan Empire.

Sub-Saharan Africa

1210–1400 .... Empire of Mali.

East Asia

618–907 .... Tang dynasty.

1236–1258 .... Mongol conquests in Middle East, Russia.

1279 .... Toppling of Sung dynasty by Kublai Khan and Mongols.

Byzantium and Eastern Europe

1054.................................Schism between Eastern and Western Christianity.

1453.................................Turkish capture of Constantinople; end of
　　　　　　　　　　　　　　　Byzantine Empire.

The Early Modern World

East Asia

1405–1433........................Great Chinese fleets.

1600–1868........................Tokugawa shogunate.

1644–1912........................Qing dynasty.

India and Southeast Asia

1498.................................Vasco da Gama (Portugal) to India.

1526–1761........................Mughal Empire.

(officially 1857)

18th century......................Mughal decline; rise of Sikh state (1708 ff.) and
　　　　　　　　　　　　　　　states of southern India.

1744, 1756–1763..............French-British wars in India.

Western Civilization

1517.................................Luther's 95 theses; beginning of
　　　　　　　　　　　　　　　Protestant Reformation.

1519–1521........................Magellan's expedition around the world.

17th century......................Scientific Revolution; Galileo (1564–1642),
　　　　　　　　　　　　　　　Newton (1642–1727).

1688–1690........................Glorious Revolution in Britain, parliamentary
　　　　　　　　　　　　　　　regime; some religious toleration; political
　　　　　　　　　　　　　　　writing of John Locke.

18th century......................Enlightenment; Voltaire (1694–1778).

Russia and Eastern Europe

1552–1556........................Russian expansion in Central Asia, western Siberia.

1689–1725........................Peter the Great and partial Westernization.

Middle East (Ottoman Empire)

1683..................................Failure of Ottoman assault on Vienna.

Latin America

1794..................................Haitian uprising against France led by Toussaint L'Ouverture; independence and end of slavery there.

The World in the First Industrial Century

Western Civilization

c. 1770..............................Invention of the steam engine by Watt; Industrial Revolution begins.

1775–1783........................American Revolution.

1789–1799........................French Revolution.

1848 ff..............................Writings of Karl Marx.

1864–1871........................German unification.

1871–1914........................Highpoint of Western imperialism.

1914–1918........................World War I.

East Asia

1839–1842........................Opium Wars in China.

1853..................................Perry expedition.

1868–1912........................Meiji period in Japan.

1894–1895........................Sino-Japanese War.

1904–1905........................Russo-Japanese War.

1911................................Chinese Revolution.

Middle East

1798................................Napoleon's Egyptian expedition.

1830................................First Ottoman reform efforts.

Latin America

1808 ff.............................Formation of governing junta in Venezuela; independence wars in Latin America.

1880 ff.............................Growing commercialization of Latin American economy.

1910................................Beginning of Mexican Revolution.

Sub-Saharan Africa

1807–1834........................Abolition of Atlantic slave trade.

1814................................Acquisition by British of Dutch South Africa.

1870–...............................Rapid European Imperialist Gains.

India and Southeast Asia

1885................................Formation of Indian National Congress.

Russia and Eastern Europe

1854–1856........................Crimean War.

1861................................Russian emancipation of serfs.

1884–...............................Beginnings of Russian industrialization; Sergei Witte leading minister; completion of the trans-Siberian railway.

1917................................Russian Revolution; abolition of the tsarist regime; Bolshevik victory.

Patterns of 20th-Century History

World Events

1919.................................Paris Peace Conference (Versailles); founding of the League of Nations.

1929–1939........................Worldwide economic depression.

1939–1945........................World War II; atomic bomb dropped on Japan.

1947–1989........................Cold War.

Western Civilization

1933–1944........................Nazi regime in Germany.

1940–1944........................Holocaust, slaughter of six million Jews.

1958.................................Founding of European Economic Community (Common Market).

East Asia

1949.................................Communist victory in China.

1978.................................More market economy in China.

India and Southeast Asia

1920.................................Beginning of Gandhi's nonviolent movement and widened efforts toward decolonization.

1947.................................India and Pakistan independent.

Middle East

1923 ff. ....Independent Turkey created by Atatürk; beginning of modernization drive; rise of independent Persia under Shah Riza Khan.

1948.................................State of Israel declared.

1980–1988........................Iran-Iraq War.

Timeline

Sub-Saharan Africa

1919 .... First meeting of the Pan-American Congress; rise of African nationalism.

1990 ff. .... Dismantling of apartheid in South Africa; several democratic elections in Kenya, other nations.

Glossary

absolutism: Concept of government developed during the rise of nation-states in Western Europe in the 17th century. Absolutism featured monarchs who passed laws without parliaments, appointed professionalized armies and bureaucracies, established state churches, and imposed state economic policies.

American exceptionalism: The idea that the United States, though emerging from a Western European background, developed novel institutions and cultural forms that constitute an exception to the European model.

apartheid: Policy of strict racial segregation imposed in South Africa to permit the continued political and economic dominance of whites.

caliphate: The political and religious successor to Muhammad.

caste system: Rigid system of social classification first introduced into the Indian subcontinent by Aryans.

caudillismo: A common form of authoritarian rule in 19th- and 20th-century Latin America.

Colombian exchange: Biological and ecological exchange that took place following the Spanish establishment of colonies in the New World. As the peoples of Europe and Africa came to the New World, animals, plants, and diseases of the two hemispheres were transferred.

consumerism: The pattern of regular acquisition and the assumption that life can be measured in part by shopping and acquiring (which accompany consumer society in many parts of the world). Usually joined by new marketing forms such as the department store.

demographic transition: Shift to low birth rate, low infant death rate, and a stable population; first emerged in Western Europe and the United States in the late-19th century.

dharma: The caste position and career determined by a person's birth. Hindu culture required the acceptance of one's social position and optimal performance of one's occupation in order to have a better situation in the next life.

divine kingship: From the postclassical period onward, many African kings claimed that they were divine and surrounded themselves with appropriate ritual, though most of them also negotiated with other groups in their kingdoms.

encomienda: Early landed estate systems in Spanish America; based on grants of Indian labor.

Enlightenment: Intellectual movement centered in France during the 18th century. The Enlightenment featured scientific advancements, application of scientific methods to the study of human society, and the belief that rational laws could describe social behavior.

feminism: This movement sought various legal and economic gains for women, including equal access to professions and higher education. The movement came to concentrate on the right to vote and won support particularly from middle-class women. Feminism was active in Western Europe at the end of the 19th century and revived in light of other issues in the 1960s.

feudalism: The social organization created by exchanging grants of land or fiefs in return for formal oaths of allegiance and promises of loyal service. Feudalism was typical of the Zhou dynasty and the European Middle Ages. Greater lords provided protection and aid to lesser lords in return for military service.

fundamentalism: The belief that religion should go back to original doctrines and ethical standards. Fundamentalist movements emerged in most major religions in the later-20th century, often associated with growing intolerance of other beliefs. Fundamentalists often used new communication devices and sometimes added new ideas to old ones.

glasnost: Policy of openness or political liberation in the Soviet Union put forward by Mikhail Gorbachev in the late 1980s.

globalization: The increasing interconnectedness of all parts of the world, particularly in communication and commerce but also in culture and politics.

hacienda: Rural estates in Spanish America producing agricultural products for markets; based on exploited peasant labor.

Harappa: Along with Mohenjodaro, the major urban complex of the Harappan civilization. It was laid out on a planned grid pattern.

Homo sapiens sapiens: The humanoid species that emerged as most successful at the end of the Paleolithic period.

import substitution: Typical of Latin American economies during the 20th century. This change involved the increase in domestic production of goods that had previously been imported, and led to light industrialization.

Industrial Revolution: A series of changes in the economies of Western nations between 1740 and the 20th century. The Industrial Revolution was stimulated by rapid population growth, increases in agricultural productivity, the commercial revolution of the 17th century, and the development of new means of transportation. In essence, industrialization involved technological change and the application of machines to the process of production.

international NGOs: Nongovernmental organizations, or NGOs, began to form international networks in the late-19th century around anti-slavery and other movements. They proliferated from the 1960s onward, concerned with such issues as human rights, environmentalism, labor conditions, and women's rights.

Marxism: Marxism emphasized the revolutionary potential of the industrial working class, which would overthrow capitalism, presumably through violent revolution, and institute a classless, free society. Labor movements in many parts of the world emphasized Marxism from the 1840s into the later-20th century.

Meiji period: The reform period that began in Japan in 1868, with rapid changes in politics and in economic and social conditions. *Meiji* means "enlightened."

Middle Kingdom: The territory in China that follows the Yellow and Yangtze rivers, usually politically united and forming the core of Chinese society from the later classical period onward.

modernization: The idea that societies around the world would move in similar directions to replace traditional structures with industrial economies, modern states, mass education, science, and other features, and the idea that these various changes would be connected. The theory is often criticized as being oversimple and unduly Western in focus.

Mughals: Dynasty established by Babur in India in 1526; the name is taken from the supposed Mongol descent of Babur, but there is little indication of any Mongol influence in the dynasty. The regime became weak after the rule of Aurangzeb in the first decades of the 18th century.

Neolithic revolution: The succession of technological innovations and changes in human organization that led to the development of agriculture.

new nations theory: The idea that many nations, when they cast off colonial rule, have characteristic problems of establishing legitimacy, maintaining internal unity and external boundaries, and dealing with new economic relationships. Government instability and/or authoritarian rule often result.

nomads: Cattle-, camel-, or sheep-herding societies normally found on the fringes of civilized societies; commonly referred to as "barbarian" by civilized societies.

Opium Wars: Fought between the British and Qing China beginning in 1839 to protect British trade in opium. The wars resulted in a resounding British victory and the opening of Hong Kong as a British port of trade.

Ottomans: Turkish-speaking people who lived in the vast Ottoman Empire, a small part of which is now modern-day Turkey. The Ottoman Empire, founded on Islamic traditions, was one of the most powerful civilizations in the modern era until its dissolution in 1918.

Pacific Rim: The region that includes Japan, South Korea, Singapore, Hong Kong, and Taiwan. It is typified by rapid growth rates, expanding exports, and industrialization; either Chinese or strongly influenced by Confucian values; considerable reliance on government planning and direction; and limitation on dissent and instability.

periodization: The device historians use to identify coherent patterns of change over time: A period begins when new dominant features are introduced, such as political independence after the American Revolution. A period ends when these features, though possibly still in play, are replaced by others in predominantly shaping the phenomenon, society, or societies in question.

Reformation: The challenge to the Catholic Church and religious unity in Western Europe that began with Lutheranism in the early-16th century. The Reformation provoked Catholic change, as well, and led to broader changes in European politics, economics, and family life.

Renaissance: The cultural and political movement in Western Europe that began in Italy circa 1400. The Renaissance was based on urban vitality and expanding commerce and featured literature and art with distinctly more secular priorities than those of the Middle Ages.

Safavids: People of the Safavid, an Iranian dynasty (1502–1736) that established Shi'a Islam as the official state religion. Safavids, a Turkish-speaking people, were descendents of a Shiite Sufi order. As a rather aggressive group, Safavids sought to advance their empire through military means.

Scientific Revolution: Culminating in the 17th century, a period of empirical advances associated with the development of wider theoretical generalizations. The revolution resulted in changes in the traditional beliefs of the Middle Ages.

Shiite: The vital minority movement that began in Islam over disputes as to who should succeed Muhammad as ruler. Shiites typically believe that theirs is a purer form of Islam and, at various times, have clashed with the Sunni majority.

shogunate: The partially centralized feudal government that emerged in Japan at several points, most notably the Tokugawa shogunate that began early in the 17th century. Shoguns were the effective rulers in this system, even though emperors were officially revered, as well.

Silk Road: The most famous of the trading routes established by pastoral nomads connecting the European, Indian, and Chinese civilizations. Goods and ideas were transmitted among civilizations along the Silk Road.

Sufism: Mystics within Islam; responsible for the expansion of Islam to southeastern Asia and other regions.

Sunni: A political and theological division within Islam.

Zoroastrianism: An animist religion that saw material existence as a battle between the forces of good and evil and stressed the importance of moral choice. In Zoroastrianism, the righteous lived on after death in the "House of Song." It was the chief religion of the Persian Empire.

Biographical Notes

Alexander the Great (356–323 B.C.E.): Successor of Philip II. He successfully conquered the Persian Empire before his death and attempted to combine Greek and Persian cultures.

Ban Chao (c. 48–117 C.E.): An influential female intellectual and writer in the Han dynasty. Her advice to women was republished in the 19th century.

Buddha (c. 6th century B.C.E.): Creator of a major Indian and Asian religion; born as the son of a local ruler among Aryan tribes located near the Himalayas. He became an ascetic, found enlightenment under a bo tree, and taught that it could be achieved only by abandoning desires for all earthly things.

Chinggis (Genghis) Khan: Born in the 1170s, in the decades following the death of Kabul Khan, and elected khagan of all Mongol tribes in 1206, Chinggis Khan was responsible for the conquest of the northern kingdoms of China and territories as far west as the Abbasid regions. He died in 1227, before the conquest of more of the Islamic world.

Confucius (c. 551–479 B.C.E.): Also known as Kung Fuzi; major Chinese philosopher and author of *The Analects*. His philosophy was based on the need for restoration of order through the advice of superior men to be found among the *shi*.

Mikhail G. Gorbachev (b. 1931): U.S.S.R. premier after 1985. He renewed attacks on Stalinism, urged reduction in nuclear armament, and proclaimed the policies of *glasnost* and *perestroika*.

Herodotus (484–425 B.C.E.): Frequently identified as the "father of history," Herodotus was a 5th-century traveler who detailed the conflict between Greece and Persia in an assortment of stories called *The Histories*. *The Histories* exemplifies Herodotus's unbiased and methodical research and writing style, on which the discipline of history has been modeled.

Ibn Battuta (1304–c. 1378): Arab traveler who described African societies and cultures in his travel records.

Kublai Khan (1215–1294): Grandson of Chinggis Khan and commander of the Mongol forces responsible for the conquest of China. He became khagan in 1260 and established the Sinicized Mongol Yuan dynasty in China in 1271.

Lao Tzu (c. 6th century B.C.E.): A major Chinese philosopher, Lao Tzu recommended retreat from society into nature. His philosophy held that individuals should seek to become attuned with the *dao*.

Mansa Musa (d. 1337): Ruler of the Mali Empire during its height, between 1312 and 1337. A devoted Muslim who built mosques throughout the empire, he sought to spread Islam by propelling its major city, Timbuktu, to global prominence.

Peter the Great (1672–1725): Son of Alexis Romanov and Russian ruler from 1689 to 1725. His reign saw the continued growth of absolutism and conquest, along with definite interest in changing selected aspects of the Russian economy and culture through imitations of Western European models.

James Harvey Robinson (1863–1936): An innovative historian of the Victorian era who taught at the University of Pennsylvania (1891–1895) and Columbia University (1895–1919). Robinson pioneered the idea behind a new type of history that stressed the multidisciplinary progress of humanity. He also sponsored a new emphasis on Western civilization in American teaching. During his distinguished career, he was president of the American Historical Association.

Socrates (469–399 B.C.E.): Athenian philosopher of the later-5th century B.C.E. and tutor of Plato. He urged rational reflection of moral decisions and was condemned to death for corrupting the minds of the Athenian youth.

Arnold Toynbee (1889–1975): A British historian whose 12-volume analysis of the rise and fall of civilizations, *A Study of History* (1934–1961), was a synthesis of world history—a meta-history based on universal rhythms of rise, flowering, and decline.

Zoroaster: An ancient Persian religious prophet who is thought to have lived around 1000 B.C. He was the founder of Zoroastrianism, a religion asserting that man had been given the power to choose between good and evil. Zoroastrianism became not only the national religion of the Sassanian Empire but also a driving force behind the entire Persian civilization. Following Alexander the Great's conquest, Zoroastrianism died out in Persia but found new life as the basis of the Parsi religion in India.

Bibliography

Essential Reading:

Adas, Michael. *Machines as the Measure of Men: Science, Technology, and Ideologies of Western Dominance*. Ithaca, NY: Cornell University Press, 1990. A careful probing of how technology increasingly shaped Western attitudes toward others; a good companion piece to the more deterministic Cipolla book (listed under Supplementary Reading, below).

Bentley, Jerry. *Old World Encounters: Cross-Cultural Contacts and Exchanges in Pre-Modern Times*. Oxford: Oxford University Press, 1993. A solid study of some of the less familiar contacts among major societies, particularly in Eurasia, from the classical period onward.

Christian, David. *Maps of Time: An Introduction to Big History*. Berkeley, CA: University of California Press, 2005. A fascinating example of "big history" from the Earth's origins onward.

Drescher, Seymour. *The Mighty Experiment: Free Labor versus Slavery in British Emancipation*. Oxford: Oxford University Press, 2004. A leading study, emphasizing humanitarian factors but dealing intelligently with other arguments.

McNeill, William. *Plagues and Peoples*. Garden City, NY: Anchor, 1998. A classic account of the role of disease in world history.

Northrup, David. *Africa's Discovery of Europe, 1450–1850*. Oxford: Oxford University Press, 2002. Provides a fresh vantage point on one of the major new encounters that began in the 15th century.

Pilcher, Jeffrey. *Food in World History*. London: Routledge, 2005. This provocative survey deals extensively with the Colombian exchange.

Stearns, Peter N. *The Industrial Revolution in World History*, 3rd ed. Boulder, CO: Westview Press, 2006. A convenient summary that focuses on global causes and consequences.

———, Erick Langer, Lily Hwa, Merry E. Wiesner-Hanks, and Paul Vauthier Adams. *Experiencing World History*. New York: New York University Press, 2000. A good introduction to issues of social inequality, gender, and population structures in the world history context.

Wallerstein, Immanuel. *The Modern World-System II: Mercantilism and the Consolidation of the European World-Economy, 1600–1750*. New York: Academic Press, 1980. This seminal work outlines and illustrates world economy theory and probes the formation of the system.

Supplementary Reading:

Abou-El-Haj, Rifa'at. *Formation of the Modern State: The Ottoman Empire, Sixteenth to Eighteenth Centuries*. Syracuse, NY: Syracuse University Press, 2005. This recent treatment emphasizes the positive and durable features of Ottoman rule.

Abu-Lughod, Janet. *Before European Hegemony: The World System, A.D. 1250–1350*. Oxford: Oxford University Press, 1991. An excellent examination of "global" trade patterns before 1492.

Adas, Michael. *Dominance by Design: Technological Imperatives and America's Civilizing Mission*. Cambridge, MA: Belknap Press, 2006. A recent comparative discussion of America's world role.

Ahmed, Leila. *Women and Gender in Islam: Historical Roots of a Modern Debate*. New Haven, CT: Yale University Press, 1993. A subtle look at a complex relationship.

Ahuja, Gurdas. *BJP and Indian Politics: Policies and Programmes of the Bharatiya Janata Party*. Columbia, MO: South Asia Books, 1994. Explores developments in Hinduism.

Akita, Shigeru, ed. *Gentlemanly Capitalism, Imperialism and Global History*. Basingstoke, U.K.: Palgrave Macmillan, 2002. Some unconventional treatments of imperialism and the world history context.

Allen, Lindsay. *The Persian Empire: A History*. London: British Museum Publications, 2004. A readable recent survey of a major classical society too often downplayed.

Allsen, Thomas. *Culture and Conquest in Mongol Eurasia*. Cambridge: Cambridge University Press, 2004. A wide lens applied to the Mongol experience and legacy.

Anderson, Benedict. *Imagined Communities: Reflections on the Origin and Spread of Nationalism*. London: Verso, 1991. The most widely cited study on the nature and origins of modern nationalism and its global role.

Antoun, Richard. *Understanding Fundamentalism*. Walnut Creek, CA: AltaMira Press, 2000. A clear and ambitious book on one of the most important cultural phenomena of our time.

Arnason, Johann P. *Axial Civilizations and World History*. Boston: Brill, 2004. The Axial Age formulation is one way to get at the basic cultural achievements of the period, and this is a good recent treatment.

Asher, Catherine, and Cynthia Talbot. *India Before Europe*. Cambridge: Cambridge University Press, 2006. A lively account of the Mughals and other early modern states and cultures in India.

Bell-Fialkoff, Andrew. *The Role of Migration in the History of the Eurasian Steppe: Sedentary Civilization vs. "Barbarian" and Nomad*. Basingstoke, U.K.: Palgrave Macmillan, 2000. An innovative look at exchanges in and around Central Asia.

Berkovitch, N. *From Motherhood to Citizenship: Women's Rights and International Organizations*. Baltimore, MD: The Johns Hopkins University Press, 2002. Discusses international women's rights movements and their impact.

Brown, Peter. *The Rise of Western Christendom: Triumph and Diversity, 200–1000 A.D.* Cambridge, MA: Blackwell, 2003. A major scholar addresses the surge of one of the leading world religions.

Carmody, Denise. *Women and World Religions*, 2nd ed. Englewood Cliffs, NJ: Prentice Hall, 1988. An ambitious look at the interaction between religion and gender.

Chadwick, Robert. *First Civilizations: Ancient Mesopotamia and Ancient Egypt*, 2nd ed. London: Equinox Publishing, 2005. A fine study that blends comparison with a sense of what early civilization was all about.

Chaliand, Gerard. *Nomadic Empires: From Mongolia to the Danube*. New Brunswick, NJ: Transaction Publishers, 2006. Puts nomadic contributions to Eurasian history in wide perspective.

Chant, Sylvia, and Nikki Craske. *Gender in Latin America*. New Brunswick, NJ: Rutgers University Press, 2003 Combines history and contemporary assessment.

Cipolla, Carlo. *Guns, Sails and Empires: Technological Innovation and the Early Phases of European Expansion, 1400–1700*, rpt. ed. Manhattan, KS: Sunflower University Press, 1985. A brief discussion of the main causes of European expansion.

Cook, Constance A. *Defining China: Image and Reality in Ancient China*. Honolulu, HI: University of Hawaii Press, 1999. A fine recent treatment, good for comparative purposes.

Croll, Elizabeth. *Feminism and Socialism in China*. New York: Schocken Books, 1988. Extremely perceptive.

Curtin, Philip, et al. *African History from Earliest Times to Independence*, 2nd ed. White Plains, NY: Longman Publishers, 2005. A distinguished account by an author team headed by a leading world historian.

Bibliography

Danzer, Gerald. *Atlas of World History*. New York: Todtri Productions, 2004. Exceptionally well done, with an eye to the geographical basis of the field.

Dear, Robert. *Revolutionizing the Sciences: European Knowledge and Its Ambitions, 1500–1700*. Princeton, NJ: Princeton University Press, 2001. Deals with one of the major shifts in the West and, ultimately, the world.

Diamond, Jared. *Guns, Germs and Steel: The Fates of Human Societies*. New York: W.W. Norton & Company, 1999. A legitimately famous study of the different economic and ecological bases of human societies.

———. *The Rise and Fall of the Third Chimpanzee: Evolution and Human Life*. London: Vintage UK, 2004. A stimulating study of the rise and decline phenomenon.

Dunn, Ross. *Adventures of Ibn Battuta: A Muslim Traveler of the Fourteenth Century*. Berkeley, CA: University of California Press, 2004. An engaging study of possibly the world's greatest traveler; illustrates a key theme of the postclassical period.

Dyer, Christopher. *An Age of Transition? Economy and Society in England in the Later Middle Ages*. Oxford: Oxford University Press, 2005. In dealing with a specific time and place, this book generates interesting findings about change and continuity in Western ideas and institutions.

Eaton, Richard M. *India's Islamic Traditions*. Oxford: Oxford University Press, 2003. Deals with a vital and complex aspect of religious interactions that began in the postclassical period.

Eklof, Ben. *Soviet Briefing: Gorbachev and the Reform Period*. Boulder, CO: Westview Press, 1989. An excellent treatment of initial moves toward democracy in the Soviet Union.

Eltis, David, et al., eds. *Slavery in the Development of the Americas*. Cambridge: Cambridge University Press, 2004. A recent collection dealing with one of the leading developments in the early modern period.

Fagan, Brian. *People of the Earth: An Introduction to World Prehistory*. Reading, MA: Addison Wesley, 1997. A good treatment of human origins, migrations, and early development.

Fernandez-Armesto, Felipe. *Millennium*. New York: Free Press, 1996. A magisterial look at 1,000 years of world history, with particular focus on transitions, such as the 15th century.

Finley, Moses I. *Ancient Slavery and Modern Ideology*, exp. ed. New York: Markus Wiener Publishers, 1998. A classic study of what slavery meant in classical contexts.

Forment, Carlos. *Democracy in Latin America, 1760–1900,* vol. 1: *Civic Selfhood and Public Life in Mexico and Peru*. Chicago: University of Chicago Press, 2003. Covers major political developments and disputes in a formative period.

Freeman, Charles. *The Closing of the Western Mind: The Rise of Faith and the Fall of Reason*. London: Vintage, 2005. A controversial look at trends in postclassical Europe.

Fukayama, Frances. *The End of History and the Last Man*. New York: Harper Perennial, 1993. A striking statement on global democracy, now somewhat dated but still provocative.

Fuller, C. J., and Veronique Benei. *The Everyday State and Society in Modern India*. London: C. Hurst & Co., 2001. An earlier and clear success story.

Gasster, Michael. *China's Struggle to Modernize*, 2nd ed. New York: McGraw-Hill, 1983. Obviously uses the modernization concept, while exploring important though not permanent impediments in 19th-century China.

Ghant, Sylvia. *Gender in Latin America*. New Brunswick, NJ: Rutgers University Press, 2002. Dealing with an important topic in its own right, this book also provides new perspectives on the Latin American experience more generally.

Gosden, Chris. *Prehistory: A Very Short Introduction*. Oxford: Oxford University Press, 2003. A readable, up-to-date account.

Gray, John. *False Dawn: The Delusions of Global Capitalism*. New York: New Press, 2000. Offers a stinging critique of globalization.

Guarneri, Carl. *America Compared: American History in International Perspective Since 1865*. Boston: Houghton Mifflin Company, 2004. Essays dealing with American developments in comparative and global contexts.

Guha, Ramachandra. *Environmentalism: A Global History*. White Plains, NY: Longman, 1999. Covers a vital facet of world history.

Hammond, N. G. L. *The Genius of Alexander the Great*. London: Gerald Duckworth & Co., 2004. A good entry into one of the major architects of key phases of the classical period in several different regions.

Hartman, Mary. *The Household and the Making of History: A Subversive View of the Western Past*. Cambridge: Cambridge University Press, 2004. A provocative look at Western distinctiveness from the angle of gender.

Hiro, Dilip. *Holy Wars: The Rise of Islamic Fundamentalism*. London: Routledge, 1989. A more balanced treatment than most.

Hobsbawm, Eric. *The Age of Extremes: A History of the World, 1914–1991*. London: Vintage, 1996. Offers a wide view of change, though with a definite European focus.

Hughes, Lindsey. *Peter the Great and the West: New Perspectives*. Basingstoke, U.K.: Palgrave Macmillan, 2001. A persuasive look at a key issue in Russian and world history.

Inglehart, Ronald. *Modernization, Cultural Change, and Democracy: The Human Development Sequence*. Cambridge: Cambridge University Press, 2005. A recent study that offers definition, data, and some defense of this intriguing but beleaguered concept.

239

Kearney, Milo. *The Indian Ocean in World History*. London: Routledge, 2003. Focuses on a crucial point of interchange in the classical period and beyond.

Khodarkovsky, Michael. *Russia's Steppe Frontier: The Making of a Colonial Empire, 1500–1800*. Bloomington, IN: Indiana University Press, 2005. Russian expansion and frontier conditions are prime topics for the early modern period.

Knechtges, David R., and Eugene Vance, eds. *Rhetoric and the Discourses of Power in Court Culture: China, Europe, and Japan*. Seattle: University of Washington Press, 2005. An interesting comparative study that also treats the Sino-Japanese relationship.

Kolchin, Peter. *Unfree Labor: American Slavery and Russian Serfdom*. Cambridge, MA: Belknap Press, 1990. A revealing analysis of the surprising parallels between Russian and American experience and the nature and consequences of change.

Landes, David. *Revolution in Time: Clocks in the Making of the Modern World*. Cambridge, MA: Belknap Press, 2000. This book, unabashedly pro-Western, focuses on a key aspect of Western technology and its global impact.

Lapidus, Ira. *A History of Islamic Societies*, 2nd ed. Cambridge: Cambridge University Press, 2002. A masterful survey of major developments since the emergence of Islam.

Lindholm, Charles. *The Islamic Middle East: Tradition and Change*. Oxford: Blackwell Science, 2002. A fine recent study.

Lipset, Seymour Martin. *America Exceptionalism: A Double-Edged Sword*. New York: W.W. Norton & Co., 1997. Treats the exceptionalist issue by comparing patterns in Canada.

Liu, Li. *The Chinese Neolithic: Trajectories to Early States*. Cambridge: Cambridge University Press, 2005. Examines the case where early civilization flowed most directly into later developments.

Lloyd, G. E. R. *Ancient Worlds, Modern Reflections: Philosophical Perspectives on Greek and Chinese Science and Culture*. Oxford: Oxford University Press, 2006. A good discussion of key aspects of two major classical cultures.

Maier, Charles. *Among Empires: American Ascendancy and Its Predecessors*. Cambridge, MA: Harvard University Press, 2006. A recent comparative discussion of America's world role.

Mann, Charles C. *1491: New Revelations of the Americas before Columbus*. New York: Knopf, 2005. Challenging insistence on the importance and variety of developments in the Americas.

Manning, Patrick. *Migration in World History*. Belmont, CA: Wadsworth Publishing, 2000. The book addresses all major periods but has some particularly useful insights on the postclassical period and migration's role therein.

———. *Navigating World History: Historians Create a Global Past*. Basingstoke, U.K.: Palgrave Macmillan, 2003. A thorough introduction to the field and its development, by a leading practitioner.

Marks, Sally. *The Ebbing of European Ascendancy: An International History of the World, 1914–1945*. New York: Oxford University Press (A Hodder Arnold Publication), 2002. Grapples with an obviously fundamental development.

Mazlish, Bruce. *The New Global History*. London: Routledge, 2006. A powerful assertion of the deep novelty of globalization.

McEvilley, Thomas. *The Shape of Ancient Thought: Comparative Studies of Greek and Indian Philosophies*. New York: Allworth Press, 2002. Another important comparative pairing on a vital facet of classical civilizations.

Moseley, Michael. *The Incas and Their Ancestors: The Archeology of Peru*. London: Thames and Hudson, 2001. Another key pre-Colombian American case, where archeology has opened new discoveries.

Mungello, D. E. *The Great Encounter of China and the West, 1500–1800*. Lanham, MD: Rowman & Littlefield, 1999. Deals with key issues in the China of the Ming and early Qing.

Murphy, Rhoads. *History of Asia*. White Plains, NY: Longman, 2005. A good study of this huge region, appropriately divided into major civilizations; applicable for later periods as well.

Nelson, B. J., and Najma Chowdhury, eds. *Women and Politics Worldwide*. New Haven, CT: Yale University Press, 1994. Does a splendid job of discussing international women's rights movements and their impact.

Parsons, Timothy. *The British Imperial Century, 1815–1914*. Lanham, MD: Rowan & Littlefield, 1999. Deals with the dominant world power of the period.

Perrin, Noel. *Giving up the Gun: Japan's Reversion to the Sword: 1543–1879*. Boston: David R. Godine, Publisher, 1995. A fascinating story of Japan's decision largely to renounce Western weaponry.

Pomeranz, Kenneth. *The Great Divergence: China, Europe, and the Making of the Modern World Economy*. Princeton: Princeton University Press, 2001. Casts new light on the vibrancy of China's economy, from the postclassical period into the 19th century; a major contribution to revisions in conventional perspectives on the Chinese role.

Porter, James I. Classical Pasts: *The Classical Traditions of Greece and Rome*. Princeton: Princeton University Press, 2005. Good focus; helps define legacies from the classical Mediterranean that can be juxtaposed with those of China.

Redford, Donald. *Egypt, Canaan, and Israel in Ancient Times*. Princeton: Princeton University Press, 1993. A careful look at one of the crucible areas for early civilization.

Riasanovsky, Nicholas, and Mark Steinberg. *A History of Russia*, 7th ed., New York: Plume Books, 2005. This comprehensive survey offers interesting observations on the Russian-Byzantine relationship.

Rublack, Ulinka. *Reformation Europe*. Cambridge: Cambridge University Press, 2005. A good recent treatment of one of the other big shifts in early modern Europe.

Sagers, John. *Origins of Japanese Wealth and Power: Reconciling Confucianism and Capitalism, 1830–1885*. Basingstoke, U.K.: Palgrave Macmillan, 2006. An important study of the causes of Japanese change, directly relevant to the comparison with China.

Schneider, Ben. *Business Politics and the State in Twentieth-Century Latin America*. Ithaca, NY: Cornell University Press, 2001. Provides a nuanced picture of economic issues, moving away from simple Third World stereotypes.

Sen, Tansen. *Buddhism, Diplomacy and Trade: The Realignment of Sino-Indian Relations, 600–1400*. New Delhi: Manohar Publishers and Distributors, 2004. An intriguing recent examination of major contacts in Asia.

Shankman, Steven. *Early China/Ancient Greece: Thinking Through Comparisons*. Albany, NY: State University of New York Press, 2003. A rare source by a scholar ambitious enough to compare two major cases, helping define aspects of the classical period.

Sharer, Robert. *The Ancient Maya*. Stanford, CA: Stanford University Press, 2005. Explores one of the most interesting cultures in what became the Americas and one in which recent findings have been particularly important.

Shotter, David. *The Fall of the Roman Republic*. London: Routledge, 2005. A solid recent look at a classic, as well as classical, topic.

Sil, Rudra. *Managing "Modernity": Work, Community, and Authority in Late-Industrializing Japan and Russia*. Ann Arbor, MI: The University of Michigan Press, 2002. An ambitious effort at comparing the two non-Western societies that launched their own patterns of change in the 19th century.

Simone, Vera, and Anne Thompson Feraru. *The Asian Pacific: Political and Economic Development in a Global Context*. White Plains, NY: Longman Publishers, 1994. One of the better studies of a major new trend.

Skocpol, Theda. *States and Social Revolutions: A Comparative Analysis of France, Russia and China*. Cambridge: Cambridge University Press, 1979. A truly sweeping effort to grapple with contemporary revolutions.

Smith, Peter H. *Democracy in Latin America: Political Change in Comparative Perspective*. Oxford: Oxford University Press, 2005. A solid analysis.

Spence, Jonathan. *The Gate of Heavenly Peace: The Chinese and Their Revolution, 1895–1980*. Harmondsworth, U.K.: Penguin, 1982. A long view of the revolutionary process by a preeminent historian of China.

Stearns, Peter N. *Consumerism in World History: The Global Transformation of Desire*. London: Routledge, 2001. Tries to place one major set of contemporary developments in context, both historically and globally.

————. *Western Civilization in World History*. London: Routledge, 2003. This short book deals with comparative issues and issues of contact in pursuing the discussion of what Western civilization was and is.

————. *World Opinion: Origins and Impact on Modern History*. New York: One World, 2005. Traces the reasons world opinion emerged historically, the effects it has had, and its limitations.

————, Michael Adas, Stewart Schwartz, and Marc Jason Gilbert. *World Civilizations*, 5th ed. White Plains, NY: Longman Publishers, 2003. One of several up-to-date textbook treatments of world history.

Stites, Richard. *Serfdom, Society and the Arts in Imperial Russia: The Pleasure and the Power*. New Haven, CT: Yale University Press, 2005. An imaginative look at key social and cultural links and problems.

Thurner, Mark, and Andres Guerrero, eds. *After Spanish Rule: Postcolonial Predicaments of the Americas*. Durham, NC: Duke University Press, 2003. The essays deal with major issues and a variety of new findings.

Tilly, Charles. *Big Structures, Large Processes, Huge Comparisons*. New York: Russell Sage Foundation, 1989. A focused discussion of what the big changes really were in the early modern West.

Vivante, Bella, ed. *Women's Roles in Ancient Civilizations: A Reference Guide*. Westport, CT: Greenwood Press, 1999. Provides ways to follow up specific features of this key topic.

Von Laue, Theodore. *The World Revolution of Westernization: The Twentieth Century in Global Perspective*. Oxford: Oxford University Press, 1989. Deals with, though probably oversimplifies, an important trend; see also Stearns 2001.

Wade, Rex A. *The Russian Revolution, 1917* (New Approaches to European History). Cambridge: Cambridge University Press, 2000. A masterful survey.

Weatherford, Jack. *Genghis Khan and the Making of the Modern World*. New York: Three Rivers Press, 2005. One of the studies of Mongol contributions that reflects and furthers new understandings of the historic Mongol role.

Williamson, Callie. *The Laws of the Roman People: Public Laws in the Expansion and Decline of the Roman Republic*. Ann Arbor, MI: The University of Michigan Press, 2005. A stimulating analysis of a major feature of Roman political culture.

Winks, Robin W., and Joan Neuberger. *Europe and the Making of Modernity, 1815–1914*. New York: Oxford University Press, 2005. A "modernist" perspective on Europe and its new global role.

Wood, Frances. *The Silk Road: Two Thousand Years in the Heart of Asia*. Berkeley, CA: University of California Press, 2003. Engaging account of the role of this major set of links over an extended period of time.

Yoffee, Norman, and George L. Cowgill. *The Collapse of Ancient States and Civilizations*. Tucson, AZ: The University of Arizona Press, 1991. An ambitious analysis, focused on early developments.

Notes

Notes

Notes